D0172496

COLUMBUS:
HIS ENTERPRISE

DATE DUE			
OCT 7 1994			
OCT 2 1995			
NOV 2 0			
DEC 1 9 2003			

DEMCO 38-297

3 1215 00084 2317

BY THE SAME AUTHOR
(until 1972, writing under the name *Hans Koningsberger*)

FICTION

The Affair
An American Romance
A Walk with Love and Death
I Know What I'm Doing
The Revolutionary
Death of a Schoolboy
The Petersburg-Cannes Express
The Kleber Flight
DeWitt's War
America Made Me
Acts of Faith
The Iron Age (forthcoming)

NONFICTION

Love and Hate in China
Along the Roads of Russia
The Future of Che Guevara
The Almost World
A New Yorker in Egypt
Nineteen Sixty-Eight, a Personal Report

COLUMBUS: HIS ENTERPRISE

Exploding the Myth

by Hans Koning

Including

Columbus in the Classroom
by Bill Bigelow

Monthly Review Press
New York

Engravings on pages 45, 54, and 89 from *America,* part IV, with illustrations
by Théodore de Bry (Frankfort, 1594); engravings on pages 85 and 86 from
Bartolomé de las Casas, *Den Spieghel vande Spaensche tyrannie* . . . (Amsterdam,
1609). These are reprinted by permission of the Rare Book Division, The
New York Public Library, Astor, Lenox, and Tilden Foundations.

Library of Congress Cataloging-in-Publication Data

Koning, Hans, 1921–
    Columbus : his enterprise / by Hans Koning ; afterword, Columbus in
the classroom, by Bill Bigelow.
        p.   cm.
    Includes bibliographical references.
    ISBN 0-85345-825-1
    1. Columbus, Christopher. 2. America—Discovery and exploration—
Spanish. 3. Explorers—Spain—Biography. 4. Explorers—America—
Biography. I. Title.
E111.K65   1991
970.01'5—dc20
[B]   90-26579
                                                                                              CIP

Monthly Review Press
122 West 27th Street
New York, NY 10001

Manufactured in the United States of America

10 9 8 7 6 5 4 3 2

CONTENTS

A 1991 INTRODUCTION

Columbus: *His Enterprise* was written and published fifteen years ago. Miraculously, it has stayed in print ever since (with slowly increasing sales). I write "miraculously" because books in the United States that see the light of day without ads or other flourishes rarely live more than a few months. Miraculously also because during all those years I have not often found sympathy or even comprehension for its point of view, its discovery that Columbus was neither a wise but misunderstood explorer nor even a brave adventurer, but (quoting my own book) "a man greedy in large and in small ways, cruel in petty things and on a continental scale." More often than not, I saw people being *surprised* at the suggestion that the traditional image of Columbus, as taught in our schools, was a political one, based on our smug and biased reading of the past.

But in the most recent years there has been a change in the air. A new generation of children—black, white, red, yellow—in our schools has been asking for a more objective, less Eurocentric, white race-oriented, teaching of history (and this book was primarily written for our high schools). I realize that the children may not have put it that way: there was simply a gut feeling that there was something terribly and terrifyingly wrong with the traditional stuff about the pious white man and the primitive savage.

Those feelings went hand in hand with our new awareness of the environment. We are discovering that the peoples whom we contemptously called "primitive" were vastly superior householders and managers of our earth than we are, and that it may be a do-or-die matter for us to learn from them in time.

As I write this, we are approaching the five hundred year mark, the quincentennial, of the fateful year, 1492, when the first Europeans, or anyway the first recorded, "modern," Europeans made a landfall in the Americas. That mark, 1992, will be an occasion of much hoopla and ballyhoo. Our politicians will hold forth about civilization, the pioneer spirit, Americanism triumphant, and Columbus the Noble Son of Italy as our first immigrant. They assume that this will please their constituents, or anyway the majority of them, and politicians think of course in terms of majorities. But I hope they are underestimating us. Possibly the occasion will become one where we finally get to grips with the false heroes and the false heroisms which for so long have burdened our history and our national character. Quite spontaneously, from Portland to New York City, there has already sprung up a wide variety of groups wanting to commemorate rather than celebrate 1492, wanting to use this occasion to ponder on "five hundred years of American history." They feel it must be made a time for introspection, and for an effort at final conciliation of the races of America.

South of the border, the myth of Columbus obviously has a

different color. In Mexico, the 12th of October is called the day of the *Raza,* the one race as it now exists there of Spanish, Indian, and African blood. Mexico City's central avenue, the Paseo de la Reforma, has statues of Aztec chiefs and Mexican heroes all along its length, with near one end a single statue of Columbus (the only one in town), which is the site of frequent anticolonial, antiracist, anti-Spanish demonstrations. The year 1992 will be commemorated in Mexico by seminars and the publication of a new history of the country, not by celebrations. In Uruguay, the Indians will commemorate October 11, 1492, as their "last day of freedom." But there are also countries such as Argentina and Peru where a small almost-pure-European elite holds most power, and here the festivities and their commercial fallout of plastic Santa Marias and such will presumably go full tilt. They'll be sponsored by Spain, which sees in the occasion a chance to promote its commercial influence in Latin America, and—somewhat surprisingly—by Japan, which has the same purpose in mind. There'll be parades and landings of facsimiles of Columbus' ships, and whatever else the ad men will think up.

You may object that there is nothing wrong with some fun flag waving and parading—but there is. When you read the story of Columbus that follows, keep in mind that you aren't reading anyone's opinion. You are reading facts of history. The year 1492 opened an era of genocide, cruelty, and slavery on a larger scale than had ever been seen before. We must finally learn to look at that past with open eyes. We must dare abandon our comfortable but false myths, for the sake of our children and their children. If we do not learn from history, we are doomed to repeat it. We must hope and try for a new harmony, for an atonement of past crimes, and discover in that way a truly new world.

1

THE ENTERPRISE OF COLUMBUS

C hristopher Columbus was what a friend of mine calls "a high-school hero." Every American child in second or third grade learns about the brave sailor, son of a Genoese weaver, who convinced the King and Queen of Spain to let him sail west. Fighting the elements and a crew who thought the earth was flat, he persisted, and with his three little ships discovered America.

After school, only people who are sailing enthusiasts or who are fascinated by geography ever come to grips with this man again. The books written for these people are hardly more critical than those written for children. They try to be scientific and unbiased about the facts of navigation and about the ideas Columbus had on geography. They do not much question the traditional approach.

And that approach is of the dashing adventurer, the fearless knight with blazing blue eyes (because American books on Columbus have the interesting habit of describing this son of the Mediterranean as looking like an Englishman or a Scandinavian), or, if you prefer, the Errol Flynn of the late-night television movie. He overcomes the doubts and fears of a stick-in-the-mud, superstitious environment. He is the first American, and what indeed could be more appropriate?

Now this may all seem perfectly harmless. Why worry about a good adventure yarn, especially if its actors lived five hundred years ago?

The answer of this book is: the high-school image of Columbus is not naive, it is false. The standard schoolbook image of Columbus is false.

This is important, for it did not get that way by chance. It is distorted in the same way that much in United States history is distorted. Our past, our present, and our future are burdened by these distortions. Thus there is nothing spoil-sport in taking a cold and hard look at what Columbus was all about.

Columbus scholars have spent much time and energy on such questions as whether his first landfall was on the island of San Salvador or another island. But that seems less important than the question of the spirit of the man and his voyages, which set such a heavy stamp on American history.

As one of the niceties now observed toward our minority groups and the third world, we no longer say that Columbus "discovered America." America was there and millions of people already lived in its lands.

Then Columbus was the first European to set foot on it. No, not even that, for the Vikings may have come first. (In all this, "European" is a polite way of saying "white man.") Columbus was the first European to put America on the map. And that he did, literally—he put it on the map of the world, for only the white race was at that time systematically trying to map the world. We have to add that Columbus put America in the wrong place, insisting to his dying day that it was part of Asia.

Still, he did it, and it is quite a claim. If he hadn't, someone else would have, soon enough; but the world is full of such ifs. He was the first, and it is one of the juicy firsts on mankind's calendar.

Having thus given Columbus once more his due as a great explorer, it is time to take a more serious look at his Enterprise. For that is what he himself called it: "La Empresa de las Indias," the Enterprise of the Indies.

It was a perfect name, for its motivating force was a search for profits.

Age of Exploration

Turning points in history do not come about by chance. In the fifteenth century, a number of events combined to ring in the great Age of Exploration. The most important of them was the conquest by the Turks of the entire East Mediterranean seaboard. This closed to Europeans the old trading and caravan routes to India and China. With the fall of Constantinople (since called Istanbul) in 1453, the Turkish Moslem Empire took control of the eastern Mediterranean. The spices, silk, and other luxury goods, the cream of European trade, were now marked up tenfold by Moslem middlemen, while pirates took their share on the side. At that same time, improvements in European shipbuilding and sailing techniques, and better compasses, made sea voyage less hazardous.

And, in those closing years of the Middle Ages, the Europeans' view of the world changed. People became less content with life as a closed circle, as a pilgrimage under the eyes of the Church to heaven or to purgatory or hell. Change, and private

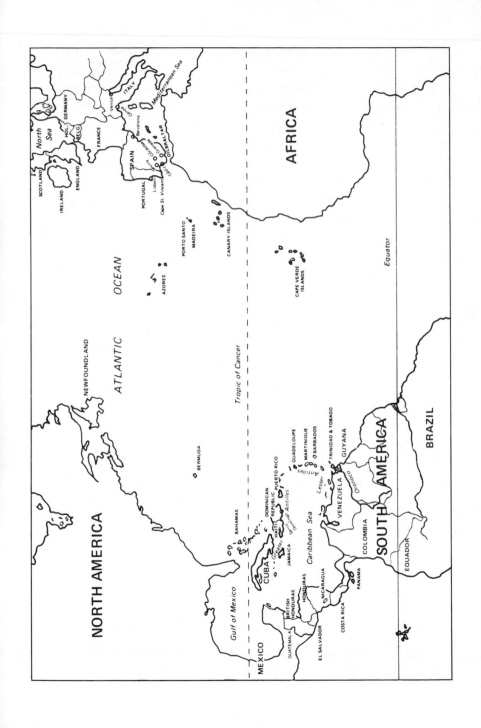

gain, were no longer dirty words. A new individualism began. At its best, it was to bring in the Renaissance, and at its near worst, early capitalism.

The land trade from the East through the Mediterranean to the West was the only important international trade at that time. The only significant profits were made from that trade. Thus, from early in the fifteenth century on, enterprising princes and merchants tried to find a way east by sea which would outflank the Moslems. Prince Henry the Navigator of Portugal was the leading force: he sent his ships south, looking for a sea route around Africa to India, each voyage venturing farther.

In 1471, eleven years after Henry's death, Portuguese ships managed to reach the equator after a grueling voyage and found that the sea there did not boil, as legend had it, and that the heat did not kill them. Sailing on, they entered another temperature zone. In 1486, Bartolomeu Diaz rounded the Cape of Good Hope. And in 1498, Vasco da Gama reached the goal, India, after a nine-month voyage round Africa— thanks to the help of an African pilot from the East African coast.

Thus it was not by chance that Spain and not Portugal (or any other country) became the sponsor of Columbus' enterprise: to try and reach India by sailing west. From the beginning of Columbus' effort to raise money, Spain had really been his only hope. For Portugal, which, as we have seen, was committed to trying the route south around Africa, had made heavy investments in that, and after 1486 smelled success.

As far as Italy was concerned, its princes had nothing to gain by any of these enterprises. Their profits still came from the Mediterranean trade with the Moslems. (But as we shall see, the bankers of Italy would prove to be less patriotic. As true early capitalists, they were prepared to go invest their money anywhere it seemed advantageous.)

And France and England, though they were approached by Columbus' brother, were not really ready for that kind of initiative. Time was running fastest around the Mediterranean: western and northern Europe were still more deeply medieval.

Only in Portugal, Spain, and the merchant cities of Italy were the spirit and the resources ready for such undertakings. Of these, Spain became the logical and unavoidable sponsor of the Columbus enterprise. It had to be Spain, moreover, of 1492, and not any earlier.

The Spain of Ferdinand and Isabella

Spain, once consisting of several small kingdoms, had become unified through the marriage of Ferdinand, king of Aragon, and Isabella, queen of Castile, whose names in Spanish are Fernando and Isabel. There were the customary battles, intrigues, and other claimants to those thrones, but from 1479 on, those two were well established as the "Catholic Monarchs," jointly ruling over the entire country. The entire country, that is, except Granada, which was at the time the last remnant of the splendid Moorish Empire, established on the peninsula by the Caliphs of Córdoba in the ninth century.

Ferdinand and Isabella consolidated their monarchy through a taming of the independent nobility and of the towns which, especially in Aragon, had been quite autonomous. As always in such cases, they were helped in their fight for power by the fact that they were waging a war against the Moors in Granada. When that long war ended with Granada's fall in 1492, Ferdinand and Isabella were solidly established. They were now ready for an alliance of their absolute monarchy with the Feudal Church and nobility.

In 1492, Spain became autocratic, theocratic, and homogeneous. It became a "modern" nation-state. After centuries of division (and religious tolerance), the last Moslem city had been conquered, and in that same year a royal decree was signed that expelled all Jews from the country.

What this new state sorely lacked was gold. Ferdinand and Isabella needed gold to overcome the financial crisis that the exodus of Jewish capital has caused, and to wage the wars they now wanted to fight in Italy for possession of the Kingdom of Naples, contested by France. The only gold Spain could earn for itself was through the export of wool. Gold then played the role of what is now "hard currency," a means of payment universally acceptable.

Ferdinand and Isabella had used the long war against the Moors to strike down the political power of the noblemen, but not their economic power. The nobility, about 2 percent of the population, owned 95 percent of the land. The peasants were not serfs: they had the right to leave their fields. But that freedom has been called "the freedom to die of hunger." There was nowhere for them to go.

The sheep of Spain, some three million of them, belonged to the *Mesta,* the sheep raisers' corporation, which was really a state within the state. Every spring, these vast flocks of sheep were driven from the high plains of Castile to the mountains of Galicia and León for summer grazing. In the fall they were brought back. They had a guaranteed free passage. The sheep walks could not be enclosed by the peasants, who twice a year saw their land despoiled and their woods cut down by the Mesta shepherds.

The wool went to Flanders for gold, and the Mesta paid no one for the damage done to the land. No one but the King, who got tax monies, and the noble owners, who reaped profits, received anything back.

This, then, is a very brief sketch of the economics of Spain at the end of the fifteenth century: half-starving peasants and noblemen holding enormous estates: townships humbly obedient to an aggressive monarchy and Church. The country was criss-crossed by millions of hungry sheep like a permanent plague of locusts. Wool was the national export but the wool trade brought in diminishing returns, and the damage to the land began causing repeated famines at home.

It was no wonder that envious eyes looked at the riches from commerce, and at the easy prosperity that the trade in spices and gold had brought to Venice, and was bringing to Portugal from its trading stations along the African coast.

The "Catholic Monarchs" felt they had a role to play in the world that could neither be financed by their miserable peasants nor by the Mesta alone. The stage was set for Columbus and the *conquistadores* who came after him.

2

THE CASE "COLUMBUS"

O f course, no amount of historical fact can explain why Christopher Columbus and no one else was determined to undertake that remarkable voyage. Many theories have been suggested: Columbus was a Jew, looking for the lost tribes of Israel, Columbus sailed because he had been in Iceland learning about the voyages of the Vikings; and so forth. These ideas are either unproven or downright silly, and none of them brings us closer to the gist of the question: why him? In some way, the elements were mixed in him—so much courage, so much stubbornness, so much knowledge, so much ignorance, so much ambition or greed—so that they added up to this man and no other. And, as always in such cases, his determination was less astonishing than his power to convince others to let him have his way.

His Background

Cristoforo Colombo (or in English, Christopher Dove) was born in or near Genoa on the Italian coast, son of the weaver Domenico Colombo and his wife Susanna Fontanarossa. The year is not certain, but 1451 is usually accepted. As a craftsman, his father had to be a member of one of the guilds, associations that brought together everyone in one craft (comparable to our trade unions). This meant he had some standing in the community. There were no middle classes then, in the modern sense of the word. But a weaver in that important trading center would have been a free towns-man, very respectful but not subservient toward his superiors (of which there were many), working according to strict rules and regulations, but owning his own loom and not working for a boss. That is all that can be said about him with any certainty.

It was a sign of the changing times that the son of such a man could go to sea and "rise through the ranks" to become his own master. That wasn't something that would happen to the son of a Flemish or an English weaver yet. Around the Mediterranean the old order of things was loosening up, and it was not quite taken for granted anymore that a son followed in the footsteps of his father.

Nothing is known about Cristoforo's childhood. Two of his brothers entered history with him: Bartolomé, who became his partner in his Enterprise, and Giacomo, much younger than the others, who also sailed with him and is known by the later Spanish translation of his name, Diego (in English, John or James). Like everyone else then, they had biblical first names. Sentimental writers have made much of the fact that our Columbus was named after Saint Christopher, the ferryman who carried Christ on his shoulders. There is no reason to think for a moment that his parents had any deep thoughts about the meaning of the name; as little as we would not expect a Peter to be like Saint Peter.

To complete the story of the names: it is a measure of Columbus' fame that his name has so many different versions in different languages. The English, Dutch, and other North Europeans know him under his Latinized name, Christopher Columbus, because the great chronicler of the discoveries was a man who wrote in Latin: Petrus Martyr, an Italian who held office in the Church in Spain, and who as a tutor to the sons of great nobles was in on all the latest news.

The French call him Colomb, the Portuguese Colom, and the Spanish and the Latin Americans, Colón. In Spanish, the translation of his first name is Cristóbal.

There was of course no Italian nation when Christopher Columbus grew up (its creation was still four hundred years off). What we now know as Italy was then a peninsula of small princedoms and city-states, often at war with each other, and Columbus' sense of belonging was linked to his family rather than to any place. He later showed the intense family loyalty of an uprooted emigrant, and he seemed at ease only with his brothers. His descendants would identify themselves with Spain, but he himself always felt a foreigner there. He was also always looked upon as foreign by the Spaniards. Such an attitude was more unusual then than it would be now. Fifteenth-century Europeans still had a sense of belonging to one Catholic Empire under one Pope.

Columbus did not go to school in Genoa and everything in our children's books about his school days is fantasy. He learned to read and write much later and was self-taught.

Indeed, it would have been most unusual for a weaver's son to go to any formal school unless he was destined for the priesthood.

His Seamanship

Most of what has been written about Columbus' early days at sea is based on speculation by people thinking in retrospect about his days of fame, and how it *should* have been. The discoverer of a great continent must have been a great man; the originator of such a voyage must have been a dashing, brilliant seaman. Thus our books tell of his voyages to England and Scotland, even aboard Scottish ships. They give him "keen blue eyes," tall stature, and reddish blond hair. Imperceptibly, he was changed into an honorary Anglo-Saxon. Descriptions of naval battles describe him as a young ship's captain.

Actually, nothing is known of Columbus' appearance, and the various existing portraits are fantasies created after his death. If his armor and other artifacts on view in the museum in Santo Domingo, in the Dominican Republic, are genuine, he was small even for his time, when average height was perhaps as much as a foot less than it is now. And not much is known of his early career besides the fact that he went on several voyages in the Mediterranean, and in between worked for his father in Genoa.

Columbus' biographers have always had trouble with his *rank*. Did he set sail as an ordinary seaman, and if so, how and when did he become an officer? Where did his money come from; how did he, as his later marriage showed, make it from seaman to "gentleman"? Something doesn't fit.

Four different conceptions of Columbus. From top left, clockwise: a sixteenth-century portrait; a painting by Lorenzo Lotto in 1512; an engraving from a portrait painted by Mariano Maella, probably in the late 1700s; an engraving from a portrait painted in 1838 by Charles Legrand, whose model was a 1596 engraving. There are more than eighty portraits of Columbus, all made after his death. None have been authenticated.

It is the British historian and geographer G.R. Crone who solved this puzzle for me. Columbus didn't muster as a seaman but as a trader. He made his voyages as a merchant's clerk, first working for others only, later investing himself. Only in that early capitalist world of the Mediterranean were the rapid transitions he went through possible. Trading, he got his connections with the Italian banking firm Spinola and DiNegri, which would be so important to him later. But his early interest in navigation and geography made him a sharp observer who learned as he sailed along.

As for his later functions, it was quite common for the commander of an expedition not to be a seaman himself. The Duke of Medina Sidonia, who commanded the Spanish Armada, had never before been out onto the ocean and got seasick when he did. Columbus was of different ilk. He had great flair for seamanship, though his sun and star observations were usually terrible. His was not an age of specialization. A merchant-owner, or any other commander, could set a course after arguing it with his captain or master pilot, and in general run things as he saw fit.

This part-time weaver's life ended in the summer of 1476, when Columbus sailed on a Genoese convoy to Flanders or the Baltic. Shortly after his ship emerged from the Straits of Gibraltar, the convoy was attacked by French armed vessels. Columbus' ship was sunk, but he was among those who succeeded in swimming ashore. This was at Lagos, just off the farthest southern tip of Portugal. From Lagos, Columbus managed to get to Lisbon, a hundred and sixty miles north, where his brother Bartolomé was working.

Thus, fate had brought him to the capital of Portugal, the very center of European navigation and exploration.

Lisbon

Reading the history of the great voyages gives me the feeling that the southern European nations have always considered ocean-going a necessary evil, a means of reaching El Dorado, the fabled City of Gold. I think love for the sea has been the exception among them. If that is so, it has not prevented Portugal from producing splendid seafarers in its day.

It was on Sagres Point, on the very last tongue of land to the southwest, jutting out from Cape St. Vincent into the Atlantic Ocean, surrounded on three and a half sides by water, that Portugal's Prince Henry the Navigator had built the tower housing his sea academy. ("The Navigator," by the way, was a nickname invented in the nineteenth century.) There the mapmakers, mathematicians, and captains came together and planned the sea route to the Indies.

After Henry's death, the center of all these activities gradually moved to Lisbon. As we have seen, the work would eventually be crowned with complete success; and in the meantime, the way stations to the Indies along the African coast brought in ivory, pepper, gold dust, and black slaves. Here Portugal erected its trading forts, the first outposts of the worldwide European system of colonies.

(Fate would have it that they were the first, and the last. In 1975, when colonialism, at least in its crude, traditional form, had given way, the ending of the military dictatorship in Portugal finally led to a liberation of those five-hundred-year-old white bridgeheads.)

Prince Henry's southern route was not the only one sailed by the Portuguese. Ships from Lisbon also reached France, England, Flanders, Holland, Germany, and the Baltic. The

Azores and Madeira had already been settled. This country of only one million inhabitants was turned to the ocean, and its astonishing marine establishment brought hundreds of foreign merchants and seamen to Lisbon.

In the year that Columbus arrived in Lisbon, Genoa's trade was declining, and a colony of Genoese entrepreneurs who had suffered from the Turkish conquests and the competition of Venice were settled there. Genoese were traditionally well received in Lisbon. Even the admiral of the Portuguese navy had once been a man of Genoa.

Christopher's brother Bartolomé was one of these, and he probably worked for a printer of charts and books of sailing directions. The publication of that material was far from easy, for while new data streamed in from all the voyages, the general policy of the time was to keep them a secret from competing towns and nations and lock them in the royal archives. Printers had a hard time getting hold of "declassified" books and maps.

In Lisbon, Columbus, helped no doubt by his brother, found new commissions as a traveling merchant. For the next few years, he sailed on Portuguese ships and visited Ireland, the Azores, and perhaps Iceland. Around 1480, back in Lisbon, he married a very fine lady, a daughter of the former captain-general of Porto Santo, the smaller of the two Madeira Islands. They settled in Porto Santo, and here Columbus' son Diego was born.

This marriage would seem a sure indication that Columbus had made his fortune, at least in a small way. Certainly, Porto Santo was then, literally, about the end of the world. Certainly, his wife's family was of Italian origin—which would have helped his suit—and she was perhaps an illegitimate daughter of the captain-general. Even so, it was an amazing alliance for a weaver's son of that time. It is an indication of the fact that Columbus had an impressive personality, something akin to what is now called "star quality."

From Madeira Columbus made more voyages, and he may have been in command at least once. He visited the trading port El Mina on the African coast, where Portugal bartered various manufactures against alluvial (river) gold that the Africans brought in; there he supposedly caught the "gold fever."

By then he must have learned reading, writing, and elements of mathematics and astronomy. It was also in those years that he taught himself some Latin, Portuguese, and Castilian, as Spanish was then (and often still is) called.

The Mind of Columbus

The newly invented printing presses of Europe had already started producing a stream of books and pamphlets: bibles and biblical texts, Books of Marvels and Books of Monsters, Classics, and astronomy and astrology (not clearly separated). Stories of real or imaginary travels were vastly popular. Sir John Mandeville's *Travel Stories,* and Marco Polo's report on his China voyage, were printed again and again. They were studied by Columbus, as was another book, which he owned (an expensive luxury then), read, and reread, making notes in the margins. This was *Imago Mundi* (*The Image of the World*) by Pierre d'Ailly or, in Latin, Petrus Ailliacus. D'Ailly, a cardinal and chancellor of the University of Paris, wrote in the early 1400s and described the earth in remarkably scientific terms. His work helped demystify the nightmarish fantasy world of the Middle Ages. (D'Ailly also predicted a revolution for the year 1789, at the eighth conjunction of the planets Saturn and Jupiter.)

It was an impressive amount of information and education that Columbus gathered this way, at sea and ashore. It was a bit of a hodgepodge of facts and fiction in which interpretations from Old Testament prophets, ambivalent quotes from the classics, and observations of sea captains carried equal weight; but the use to which he would put all this material was a scientific and practical one. Columbus stood exactly on the borderline between two eras: he took medieval cosmography from the library to the ocean.

What interested and obsessed him was precisely the "image of the world." Everything ever written or drawn on a map was used by Columbus to prove one specific thesis about that image.

Destiny or chance certainly played a strong role in Columbus' life. A disaster at sea had brought him to the center of Western navigation. Now, when he was quietly established as a married man of property, a colossal error led him on to the great drama of his life.

This error was his belief that from the western shores of Europe to the eastern islands off Asia was "but a short voyage." Instead of east, around hostile land, or south, around Africa, the natural way to Asia was: west.

The fact that Columbus' home in those days was not on the continent but a full five hundred miles farther west on the Madeira Islands must have played a psychological role in his concept of the world. He was not the first to think this way, but only because he was so terribly wrong about the size of our earth did he go on insisting that it could be done: that Asia could be reached by sailing across the Atlantic.

The Size and Shape of the World

The traditional story, that everyone or almost everyone in those days thought the earth was flat, and that they all laughed at Columbus, who said it was round, is nonsense. It is also a painful banalization of history. (It is repeated in all our school books, including such ambitious ones as *The Story of Christopher Columbus* by Nina Brown Baker, and Macmillan's Social Studies series.)

The Greeks knew, five hundred years before Christ, that the earth is a sphere. Eratosthenes, in the third century B.C., actually determined its circumference with amazing accuracy by measuring the north-south distance between two points whose latitudes he knew. (Latitude is the distance of a place from the equator measured in degrees; from the South or North Pole to the equator is ninety degrees.) Hipparchus, a hundred years later, found a way to determine the latitude of a place by observing the sun on any day of the year, and not just during the four special positions of the sun on March 21, June 21, September 21, and December 21, as had been known until then. He drew up the first tables of the sun's height at noon, "declination" tables which make this possible. Ptolemy, working in our second century in Alexandria, added degrees of longitude to his beautiful map of the world. (Longitude is the distance in degrees measured from a north-south circle, or meridian. The Greenwich meridian is the modern-day, arbitrary line of location for measurement on the earth's surface.) He counted east from the Canary Islands, which he placed "at the end of the West."

All this knowledge, and much more, had got lost during the "Dark Ages," roughly the period from 500 to 1200 A.D. But by Columbus' day most of it had been restored to the West.

Some had come back through the scholars of Constantinople, fleeing after the fall of their city; some reached Spain and Portugal through the mediation of Arab scholars. In the 1480s there was no educated man or woman who did not know that the world was round.

As in antiquity, the earth was supposed to consist of one vast ocean in which the land mass of Europe, Africa, and Asia floated like a huge island. The medieval idea that Jerusalem was the precise middle of this round land mass had been abandoned. It was known that Asia stretched over many more degrees of longitude than Europe. There were also many stories and myths about islands lying in the ocean beyond the Azores and the Canaries, and about "balancing" countries on the other side of the earth.

Why then, on a round world, was the idea of going to the Indies the other way around so extraordinary?

Two reasons stopped captains from setting out for Asia by turning their stern to the land and going west across the ocean. The basic, almost emotional one was that no one sailed that way. Ships hugged coastlines, no matter how much of a detour that route might entail. Navigational aids were simply not trusted enough to do otherwise. Man's psychology was against it. The ocean was the unknown. And there are quite recent examples of this mentality. The first passenger flights, by KLM around 1920, went from Amsterdam to London but didn't cross the North Sea in a straight line; the pilot followed the railroad to Calais, crossed the Channel, and followed the rails to Croydon.

The second reason no one had tried sailing west to Asia was an impeccable one. The distance was too great. From the Azores to Japan is roughly ten thousand nautical or sea miles, or something like sixty million feet. No ship of that time could carry supplies for that distance, even under the best of conditions.

But Columbus believed, and managed to make others believe, that it was really only a quarter that far—that is to say, about 2,400 sea miles. (A sea mile is 1.15 times longer than our everyday statute mile.)

To reach his figure, Columbus had first of all reduced Eratosthenes' precise measure for the girth of our planet by about one-quarter. Books of the time often talked about miles and other units of length without bothering to define them, and by some sleight of hand with Roman and Arabic miles, Columbus reached the conclusion that a degree of longitude at the equator was not sixty but forty-five nautical miles. His earth had a circumference that was only three quarters of the real one.

That error would have reduced the voyage to 7,500 miles; the next error was the size of Asia. On Columbus' mental map, Cipango (Japan) did not lie at roughly 140 degrees east, but stretched another 100 or 110 degrees farther towards Europe. This deduction was based on such authorities as Aristotle, who never left the Greek world, and Marco Polo, who had measured the road from Venice to Peking with his own steps and thought it much longer than it is.

But if one single item was responsible for firing Columbus' mind, it was the Toscanelli record. Paolo Toscanelli was a Florentine philosopher, which at that time meant he was a person interested in all sciences. Toscanelli had a map based on Marco Polo's estimates of distances in Asia. Already in the year 1459, he approached King Alfonzo of Portugal with it and invited him to try a western route to the Indies. In 1474, as a very old man, he sent this map with a letter to a friend, Ferñao Martinez, a churchman in Lisbon. He urged Martinez to go to the new King John (João) of Portugal and show him how rewarding it would be to organize a voyage to Japan and China by sailing due west. Japan, Toscanelli wrote, was full of gold. (The organizers of these plans never worried about how to get the gold out of the hands of the heathens; it seemed natural to them that it would go to the Christians.)

This correspondence from the mid-1470s came to the attention of Columbus around 1480, when he was established in Madeira. Perhaps he read it in the royal archives in Lisbon, where it had been filed and forgotten. This was it! He must have felt like a man enlightened in a dark world. The shortcut to Asia lay west. (The notion that Columbus himself then wrote to Toscanelli is probably a fantasy or mistake of his son.)

It is typical of the self-taught person, even in our days, to have a fanatical capacity to latch on to one idea and blissfully ignore conflicting evidence. I do not mean this all negatively: such one-idea people move the world. And it must also be added that in those days most science consisted of a mixture of inspiration, intuition, and fact. But note that Columbus never mentioned Toscanelli again until much later. Sailing west to Asia had to be his God-given idea, and no one else's.

3

THE SELLING OF THE
WESTWARD PASSAGE

It was unthinkable to undertake such an enterprise without government support—that is to say, without a king or prince behind it. The first monarch Columbus approached was, naturally, the King of Portugal, John II, a nephew of that same Henry the Navigator who had started it all. At just about that time, in the 1480s, King John himself sent some sea captains west. Their mission was not to go all the way to Asia, but to discover the (imaginary) island of Antilia in the middle of the Atlantic. King John may actually have been inspired in this by the Toscanelli papers.

The men sent to find Antilia came back reporting empty sea. We will later see why they did not succeed. Nonetheless, John didn't say no to Columbus, but let him present his case to a commission (a device as popular then as now for postponing decisions). The commission very justly said that Columbus obviously didn't know how big the earth was.

This sequence of events shows up another favorite myth woven around Columbus: that the King of Portugal stole his idea and secretly tried to execute it himself. Columbus had not been the first to think of sailing west. Even if he had, it is not the kind of idea you can take out a patent on; it was precisely an indication of his strong personality that in the end his plan was not only accepted, but that he himself was allowed to try and execute it.

At about the time the Portuguese royal Court turned him down, early in 1485, Columbus' wife died. The two shocks must have combined to make him decide to go and try his luck in Spain. For he was by now committed to his idea with body and soul, and he never seems to have contemplated going back to ordinary seafaring and trading, not even while biding his time. It is safe to assume that from then on, Columbus was in a fever to show the world that he was right, and that no matter how poor his chances seemed, he simply didn't have the patience to engage in anything else. And he was luckier than most discoverers or inventors in that he found enough interest in his plan to allow him to stay with it. The King and Queen of Spain, whom he pursued with his scheme for the next five or six years, tried his patience, but they paid him a stipend during most of that time, an option on his services as it were. That was not an ordinary achievement, considering he was a commoner and a foreigner, and the country, Spain, very poor and at war with the Moors. This is one more indication that Columbus was a very good talker. Actually, those years may have been the most stimulating in his life.

Columbus left Portugal in the spring of the year 1485 and sailed to Spain with his son. He landed at the Río Tinto, at the port of Palos de la Frontera, the same place from which he would eventually set out on his voyage. Near this town of "Palos of the Frontier" stood a Franciscan monastery, and at some point he left his son Diego there as a boarder. Then, and later, the Franciscans helped him with introductions to important people.

Even in that religious and bigoted age, Columbus stood out as a very fierce Catholic. When he discussed his westward voyage, he always dwelt on its religious aspects: to convert the Asian "heathens" to Catholicism, and/or to use their gold for the reconquest of the Holy Land from the Moslems. In the end, the "heathens" he did find were not converted (they were killed or enslaved), and wherever the loot may have gone, it certainly was not used to take Jerusalem from the unbelievers. This does not mean that Columbus was trying to fool his backers. He must himself have believed that his Enterprise was Christian, if only to ensure God's help; and the priests who came west later were, with one or two glorious exceptions, as quick as he was in forgetting those pious intentions. (In a similar way, modern corporations used to capture oil fields and mines in underdeveloped nations while telling us and themselves that their main interest in these enterprises was to protect those unhappy countries from communism.) Anyway, the Christian coloring of his plan gave Columbus the support of many powerful Church people and played a role in the final acceptance of his Enterprise.

It seems that Columbus eventually found ship owners willing to listen to him, but when he came to realize that he couldn't do anything without royal support, he installed himself in Córdoba amidst the colony of Genoese there. The Spanish royal Court was always on the move from one town to another, and he waited for its return to Córdoba, which was not far from the military frontier of the besieged Moors of Granada. In May of 1486, he got his first audience with the King and Queen.

In the biographies of famous men and women it is often

very difficult to pin down that crucial little step that lifts them from the anonymous crowd, the step that is the most difficult of all. Columbus is no exception. For it is not clear at all why the Spanish Court should have bothered to receive an unknown veteran of a number of unimportant Portuguese voyages. True, the Court was then more accessible than in its later days of the Absolute Monarchy, but it was not customary for commoners to be received in audience. Once in, Columbus' personality made its impression, but how he got in remains a puzzle. It may have been the fascination he exerted on the Franciscans, combined perhaps with staking his savings on bribes for some chamberlain.

In he got, though, and that was more than half the battle. It is no myth that he made an impression on the Queen, and after that, with enough patience, he was bound to get help. He needed, after all, but two or three small ships. His plan was wild, but he did speak the language they wanted to hear: almost *anything* was worth a try in order to catch up with Portugal in the race to the Indies.

Columbus' Conditions

It gives another insight into the character of the man that Columbus certainly did not go hat in hand. From the beginning of his Spanish negotiations, he asked for enormous rewards in case he should succeed in his plan.

Here, too, it seems logical to assume that his motives were mixed. Part of it must have been what is now called "salesman's psychology": the more expensive you make yourself, the more the world is inclined to take you seriously. But it also shows that he had probably by this time convinced himself that his plan was unique, and that he was uniquely destined to carry it out.

In Portugal, all this could only have ruined his chances and it possibly did, if he ever had a serious chance there. For Portugal was solidly in the exploration business, and with the experience of decades, the King granted his sailor-explorers only modest, though reasonable rewards.

To Spain this was all new. The Spanish monarchs in those years must have felt that they had very little to lose; if they granted a man 10 percent, or even more, of all the riches he found, the remaining part was still (in modern terms) so much gravy. Once Spain also became experienced in the field, Columbus' terms were quickly cancelled.

What were these extravagant terms? Right from the start, Columbus asked for no less than one-tenth of all the wealth that would arrive from Asia along the new route, brought not only by himself but by everyone else, and not just for any specific period of time, but forever more, for himself and his heirs. He also wanted to be ennobled, to receive the titles of "Viceroy" and "Admiral of the Ocean Sea," and other honors and profits of similar scope. The "Admiral" title alone was an hereditary one and would have given him jurisdiction in a large part of the western Atlantic and a share in all prize money from that area, that is, in all proceeds from naval booty.

The result of Columbus' audience was another commission, or maybe just a request, from the Queen to her confessor, Hernando de Talavera, to discuss the westward plan with some learned colleagues. Talavera and his fellow philosophers first considered it around the end of that year, 1486. In that day and age, there was nothing peculiar about such a delay. (If we want to be very kind, we may think that nowadays things are done faster in government circles, though I doubt it.) No conclusion was reached, but the waiting was sweetened for Columbus with a yearly stipend of 12,000 *maravedis*.

A maravedi was by then mostly a money of account—that is to say, the actual coin had almost vanished but it was used for bookkeeping. It was worth (in gold) a bit more than half a penny of the American gold dollar of fading memory. The stipend was eighty dollars gold. What did it buy? It was about twice the yearly wages of Sancho Panza (who was fed by his master Don Quichote, though), and enough to buy two hundred bushels of wheat. No riches, but sufficient to survive on a penurious scale. Clearly, Columbus had some means of his own, for since he was taken seriously by the Court, they could hardly have wanted him to live in the style of a servant.

To Portugal and Back

The stipend did not make Columbus patient, however. In 1488 we find him back in Lisbon where he approached King John II once more.

John gave him a better reception than the first time around. Bartolomeu Diaz, trying the southern route to the Indies, had been gone seven months and was believed by many to have perished. But the negotiations with Columbus dragged, and then, in the winter of that year, Diaz returned to Lisbon in triumph, announcing that he had made it. He had rounded the Cape of Storms, as he had baptized the southern point of Africa, and the sea route to the Indies lay open. King John renamed that cape the Cape of Good Hope and decided to stick with the southern route around Africa. (It would be another ten years before Vasco da Gama actually reached India.)

Columbus, thus rejected once more, returned to Spain and the Talavera commission, while from Lisbon his brother Bartolomé, henceforth also totally committed, traveled to England and France, vainly appealing to their kings for support.

Queen Isabella took notice of the return of Columbus, and he received a royal letter that provided him with free food and lodging on his way back to the Court, where he presented himself once more. There are no data on what Chrisopher did with his time during the years of waiting that followed.

It was 1490 before Talavera sent in his final report. It said that the westward-to-Asia plan must appear impossible to any learned person because the ocean was very much wider than Columbus supposed. And so it was, of course; if there had been no America, Columbus would have perished long before reaching Japan. Isabella, however, using her royal prerogative to be illogical, told Columbus he could apply for help again when the war against the Moors of Granada had been won.

Thus, another year rolled by, presumably spent by Columbus writing angry letters to the men who did not believe him.

Toward the end of 1491, the war against the Moors was drawing to a close. Columbus traveled to the Court, which had set up headquarters in Santa Fe, almost under the walls of Granada, to wait out the end. In January 1492, the Moslem defenders of the city opened its twenty gates and surrendered. The Spanish armies streamed in, and their soldiers gaped at the marvels of the Caliphate, the Alhambra, the Court of Lions, the fountains, and the ornamented street lamps. An episode in Iberian history had come to an end.

The Agreement

The bargaining that now followed between Columbus and the Court was no doubt less whimsical and emotional than that described in the traditional accounts. In these, Columbus leaves in a sulk, is sent for, returns; there are yeses and noes as in a bazaar, and the Queen even throws her jewels on the table. G.R. Crone has deduced what really happened. There were no sudden changes of heart, and Columbus' eyes, blue or brown, played no role.

Italian bankers, much of whose activities were blocked by the Turks, were the financiers for a big part of ocean-borne trade. There was a Genoese commercial colony in Seville and local links with the Italian banking house of Spinola and Di Negri, Columbus' old employer. Francesco Pinelli, a Genoese banker of Seville and co-director of the Santa Hermandad, the Spanish state police, guaranteed a loan for the Columbus plan. Pinelli's fellow police director was none other than Luis de Santangel, the royal treasurer. The delays were probably caused because the bankers checked in Florence, using the Toscanelli papers, which had been inherited by his nephew, and got a positive report on the feasibility of the plan.

Thus a loan of 1,140,000 maravedis was provided, somewhat over $7,000 in pre-1934 gold. Conveniently, Pinelli and de Santangel also steered a police fine imposed upon the town of Palos toward the expedition.

In April 1492, the so-called Capitulations were signed, in which Columbus got all he had asked for.

He was to be given three caravels for his expedition. A caravel was a small, fast ship of the period, quite seaworthy, and lateen-rigged, that is to say, with triangular rather than square sails, held out by long, tapering yardarms. He was to

A full-scale model of the Santa Maria.

get money for a crew and supplies. He was to get his 10 percent of whatever trade was drummed up, an admiralty over the western ocean, and governorship over any newly found land. He received a royal passport and three letters from the King and Queen, one to the Grand Khan and two others to princes whose names he could fill in as the need arose. Kublai Khan, the Grand Khan, had been the Tartar ruler of China in the days of Marco Polo. That period had ended more than a hundred years earlier, but no one in Europe had been there since or was aware of that.

Columbus had achieved his end.

Let us sum up the situation in that spring of 1492. Based on the knowledge of the day, the Talavera conclusion that the westward voyage could not be achieved had been right. Probably King Ferdinand agreed, while Isabella, aware of the relativeness of all such wisdom, decided they should let the man try anyway. He seemed so sure of himself and so readily invoked God's name and inspiration in the plan, and he quoted the sages from Seneca to the Prophets in its support.

Much of the cost was guaranteed by the Genoese bankers. Wages were never paid very promptly anyway; the fine on Palos would pay for two of the three ships. Even in those frugal days, the monarchs had little to lose.

When that has been said, the fact remains that they did not only accept the plan itself but also Columbus' terms. They agreed—if he turned out to be right—to ennoble this lowly weaver's son and to make him potentially as rich as any grandee of Spain. They might not have done this if there had been a more likely candidate around, say a gentleman adventurer with family connections at Court, willing to lead such an expedition. And, anyway, the Italian bankers behind the loan probably preferred a simple compatriot over a fanciful Spaniard. However that may have been, Columbus had now become totally identified with the plan to go west to Asia.

No one else appeared eager to push him aside.

A voyage into the unknown, the willful turning of a ship's bow away from a coastline and into the open ocean, was an unheard-of act.

4

THE VOYAGE

The story of the preparations for the great voyage and of the three ships is simple enough and has been told a hundred times. Palos de la Frontera, though dragging its feet, paid the fine imposed for some act of disobedience we do not know, by providing two caravels. A third ship was chartered from its owner on the spot.

That last one was the Santa Maria, on which Columbus would sail, while her owner remained on board too. It was the largest of the three, with a length of perhaps a hundred feet, and a carrying capacity of maybe ten thousand liquid gallons or one hundred tons. The other two, the Niña and the Pinta, were no longer than about seventy feet. The names of eighty-seven of the crew members have been preserved: thirty-nine for the Santa Maria, twenty-six for the Pinta, and twenty-two for the Niña. Martin Pinzón captained the Pinta, and his brother Vicente Pinzón the Niña; without the help of the Pinzón family, who were prominent in Palos, Columbus would probably never have been able to find complete crews. That does not detract from his role as the catalyst and promoter; but a lawsuit between the Pinzón and Columbus families about credit for the discoveries trailed on for many years of the following century. Most of the crew were local men, professional sailors and not jailbirds as some stories have it. Their pay was about 1,000 maravedis per month, but it was not unusual for ship's owners to be a year or more in arrears with paying out wages. A bosun or carpenter could have earned twice as much.

Other men aboard the expedition were royal clerks whose task it was to record what happened and register any wealth taken aboard, and one man who spoke Hebrew and Arabic. He was going to be the interpreter upon arrival in Asia. . . .

It is well to remember, as an antidote to romantic sea tales written in warm libraries, that ships were then floating slums and floating sweatshops. The common fate of crew and officers gave a certain solidarity that would not have been found on land among such disparate men, but they were still masters and servants, and no nonsense. The captain was lord over life and death, and any man who evoked his displeasure could be lashed, locked in irons, keelhauled, or hanged. The food for the crew was vile—though on a normal voyage probably no worse than what they were used to on land. As for their quarters, there weren't any. The men simply had to bunk down for the night wherever they could find a dry spot, which is not easy on a sailing boat; and those who had one change of dry clothes with them were the fortunate ones.

Those were the men who did the work, though. It has been said that the great explorers of Africa were simply the first white men carried around that continent by blacks; likewise, those famous captains were the first men sailed across the oceans by their crews. At a time when a gentleman could still win fame and fortune by his daring on the ocean, the fishermen of Rouen and St. Malo were already making *two voyages a year* to the banks off Newfoundland as a matter of course, staying at sea for months of fishing without ever taking shelter on land.

It took Columbus some months to get the ships ready and to find the ninety-odd men willing to risk their skins. The ship chandlers (traders in marine stores) caused the usual delays and delivered the usual percentage of shoddy goods. On Friday, August 3, 1492, the three ships weighed anchor and sailed down the river Tinto.

Ferdinand and Isabella bidding Columbus goodbye. An engraving by Théodore de Bry, published in 1594.

These and the other famous dates of the voyage are from the Julian calendar, then in use. We now use the Gregorian calendar, created by Pope Gregory XIII, which is (almost) precisely in tune with the sun. The Julian calendar was dated from Julius Caesar and it was by Columbus' time ten days ahead of the sun. When he sailed, it was "really" July 24, while they would see land not on the 12th but on October 2, 1492.

The Crossing

The history of the conquest of America by Europeans was very much determined by natural factors. Summer and winter, the northeast tradewinds blow steadily from Spain to the Caribbean over a strip of ocean stretching from the doldrums (an area of little wind on or above the equator) to the Tropic of Cancer. Above the Tropic, the westerlies blow from the American coast to Europe, where they bend south. Those two systems of winds thus form a flattened circle.

That circle of wind was destined to blow the Spaniards and Portuguese to South and Central America, which became Latin colonies. It led the English, Dutch, and French ships (with considerably more trouble) to North America, which became English, Dutch, and French.

Columbus made it because he was the first captain to steer far enough south to pick up the northeast tradewinds; the ships King John of Portugal had sent out had been fighting westerlies on an empty ocean until they had to return. Undoubtedly, if there had been no Columbus, the ships of Portugal would eventually have reached America. Then the first landings would have been farther south; in all probability, the first ship would have touched the coast of Brazil on its way to the Cape of Good Hope. Portuguese sailors had already learned that they had more favorable winds if they did not follow the coast of Africa closely, and they had begun to dare holding ever farther out to sea. The "gap" in longitude between Brazil and Africa would presently be bridged almost by chance.

How did Columbus know to set course for the Canary Islands first, and only then give his course as due west? Several reasons come to mind. The first one was no doubt his luck— for in matters of navigation he was consistently lucky. Second, he may on his African voyage or voyages have noted the reliability of the northeastern at that latitude and worked it into his great plan. Third, the Canaries are at twenty-eight degrees north, and that, Columbus thought, was the latitude of his destination, Japan (actually, Japan lies ten degrees farther north.)

That third consideration was crucial in an age that knew, roughly, how to measure latitude by "shooting" the sun or the polestar, but that had no way at all to measure longitude, that is, east-west distance from a chosen meridian. This problem of determining longitude at sea was not licked until three centuries later, through John Harrison's chronometer. (Harrison's chronometer kept time so precisely that comparison with noon on the ship—the sun in zenith—with the hour of Greenwich gave longitude: one minute difference meant one degree east or west of Greenwich.) Columbus simply planned to stick to the twenty-eighth parallel and sail west until he hit Japan, supposedly less than three thousand miles away.

Last, and most important, the Canary Islands, of all the islands off the continent, were the only Spanish colony. Thus, they were a natural last staging place. Though Spain and Portugal were at peace, this expedition, planned to take the wind out of Portugal's sails, could not very well leave from a Portuguese possession, such as the Azores.

It took the fleet about ten days to reach the Canaries, and here some refitting took place. They picked up fresh water and other supplies. On September 6, the ships sailed from Gomera, the farthest west of the archipelago. Only two days later did they lose sight of land and enter the unknown ocean: to my mind, the most dramatic and certainly the purest moment of the Enterprise. Mankind then had no faster means of traveling than the sailing ship, and these ships were leaving their world behind at all possible speed.

Columbus' log of the month of sailing that took him to the Caribbean has disappeared, but a digest of it, made by Bartolomé de las Casas, tells us everything we might want to know. (De las Casas was that famous friar, later bishop, who came to the Indies and wrote their classical *History*. He was one of the very few churchmen to protest the treatment of the local population by the Spaniards, a protest to which he devoted his entire life. More about him later.)

The log was a bare summing up of distances sailed and weather. Speed had to be arrived at by guessing, for the log line had not yet been invented. Course was given by the compass. Speed, of course, and time (measured with an hourglass) gave an approximation of the ship's position: what is called "dead reckoning."

Sea currents had to be guessed at, too, and the magnetic variation of the compass needle, roughly measured by observation of the polestar, caused Columbus many worries.

But the weather was usually splendid, "like Andalusia in spring," Columbus frequently wrote. "Only the nightingales are missing." The tale of the double logs is well known: how Columbus kept one log for himself and one with a much lesser distance to show the crew. The two other captains and the pilot kept their own logs and all sums came out different. Actually, Columbus' false log, with the distance from Spain pared down so as not to upset the crew, came closest to the real mileage sailed.

There were certainly increased mutterings and protests among the men as the days wore on. Not because they thought they'd fall off the earth, but because this was the longest voyage out of land's sight for all of them, and the steady wind from the northeast made them feel they would never be able to sail back home. They were reassured when they ran into strong southwesterly seas one day. Columbus, without any false modesty, noted in his log that God had not given such a sign since the day he parted the Red Sea for Moses. Columbus' luck was to drive him north for his return to Spain on the westerlies. After that, he and his successors learned to sail west on the tradewinds, east and home on the westerlies. Or maybe it was not luck but his flair as a sailor. Of course, luck only favors those who are ready to appreciate it.

By the beginning of October the ships had passed the meridian of sixty degrees west and were, unbeknownst to them, quite near to what are now named the Antilles and Puerto Rico. There were now ever increasing and unmistakable signs of nearby land, such as floating branches, sticks, and great flocks of birds. The log for one of the last days, October 10, says that the men complained of the length of the voyage, and that Columbus "held out high hopes of the gains they could make" and said that there was no point in complaining "because he had [already] reached the Indies and must sail on, until with the help of Our Lord he discovered land."

The story is dramatic enough without the added details of

the supposed ultimatum from the crew and Columbus' promise that he would go back in three days if there was no land, and that, lo and behold, on the third day, there it was. It is also worth noting, for the sake of historic truth, that the two other captains, the brothers Pinzón, played a large role in encouraging the men to hold on.

In every story ever written about this voyage, the reader, not unnaturally, is made to root for the three ships. Will they make it or won't they? We share their fears and perhaps envy their courage. I, the writer of this particular report, love the sea and respect the courage of all sailors. But knowing what came after this voyage, I now find myself reading the log of those late days at sea with very different eyes. For me they acquire the drama of the murderer coming ever closer to his unsuspecting victims. There is nothing contrived about this, nothing "political." It may be dismissed by some as a bleeding-heart attitude. Indeed, our hearts should bleed for the people of the Caribbean, whose destiny was hanging in the balance those fateful last days.

It was a beautiful early autumn. The log keeps noting how the sea is "as smooth as a well," "as calm as the river at Seville." Vast flocks of birds cross the sky; songbirds land on the ships and sing from the rigging. The wind carries the scent of flowers and herbs. To what were then, to most of their population, blessed islands, the three ships were approaching as Harbingers of Death.

Land

It is painful to note that the discoverer did a sailor out of the royal reward for first sighting land. That sailor, known to be a man called Juan Rodríguez Bermeo, or Rodrigo, in the log, was aboard the Pinta, which was the fastest ship and was sailing ahead of the others. Rodrigo called "Land!" on October 12, very early in the morning, when he saw the moon shining on the cliffs or the white sandy beach of an island now called Watlings, or San Salvador, in the Bahamas.

Rodrigo thus earned himself a yearly pension of 10,000 maravedis for the rest of his life—or so he thought. Columbus, claiming that he had seen a light on the evening before, said he himself was the first man and that the reward was his.

Columbus and the other two captains went ashore in an armed boat, and amidst a crowd of what would henceforth be called Indians, and with the royal scribe as witness, Columbus announced that he was taking possession of those lands for the King and Queen of Castile (although he assumed he was in the realm of the Japanese emperor).

Bartolomé de las Casas, describing all this from the log, then quotes Columbus' own words about his impressions of the Indians. The words should be repeated here, with a view to what he said and did later.

"To win their friendship," Columbus wrote in his log, "and realizing that here was a people to be converted to our Holy Faith by love and friendship and not by force, I gave some of them red caps, glass beads, and many other little things. These pleased them very much and they became very friendly. They later swam out to the ship's boats in which we were seated, and brought us parrots and balls of cotton and spears and many other things, which they exchanged for the glass beads and hawks' bells. They willingly traded everything they owned. But they seemed to me a poor people. They were all naked as the day they were born, the women too, although I saw but one young girl." (At another place in the log, as if to reassure his sovereigns, Columbus tells them that all the gifts he made to one particular man, a red cap, a string of glass beads, and two hawks' bells, were together worth less than three cents.)

"All the men looked young, under the age of thirty. They were well built, with good bodies and handsome features. Their hair is coarse, like horse's hair, and short; they wear it down in a fringe and with some strands at the back. They have the same color as the Canary Islanders, as they are at the same latitude. They do not bear arms, and do not know them, for I showed them a sword, they took it by the edge and cut themselves out of ignorance. They have no iron. Their spears are made of cane. . . . They would make fine servants, and they are intelligent, for I saw that they repeated everything said to them. I believe they could easily be made Christians, for they appeared to have no idols. God willing, when I make my departure I will bring half a dozen back to their Majesties, so that they can learn to speak." (Spanish, he presumably meant.)

And later, "I saw two or three villages, and their people came down to the beach calling to us and offering thanks to God. Some brought us water, others food, and still others jumped in the sea and swam out to us. We thought they were asking if we came from the heavens. One old man got into the boat, and the others, both men and women, cried, 'Come and see the men who have come from heaven, and bring them food and water.' Many men and women came, each bringing a gift and offering thanks to God. They threw themselves on the ground and pointing at the sky, called us ashore. . . . I went to view all this in the morning, to give an account to your Majesties and to see where a fort could be built. I saw a kind of peninsula with six huts. It could be made into an island in two days, though I feel no need to do this, for these people are totally unskilled in arms, as your Majesties will learn from seven whom I had captured and taken aboard, to learn our language and to take them to Spain. But, should your Majesties command it, all the inhabitants could be taken away to Castile, or made slaves on the island. With fifty men we could subjugate them all and make them do whatever we want."

Bartolomé de las Casas, in the first book of his *History of the Indies,* adds to this, "Two things should be pointed out, first, the natural willingness and readiness of these people to receive our Holy Faith, and their readiness to accept Christianity and morality, if treated with love, charity, and kindness; and how welcome that would have been to God; and secondly, how far the Admiral [i.e., Columbus] was from the proper observation of divine and natural law, and how little he understood the duty of the King and Queen and of himself toward these natives, as he so lightly could say that they might take all these Indians, the natural inhabitants of these lands, to Castile or make them slaves on their own island, etc. This was very far from the purpose of God and His Church, to whom this voyage and the discovery of all this world and everything in and about it should have been dedicated. . . ."

However, these Indians were destined not even to live as slaves; they were to die. And no other man in that Church which de las Casas mentions here, and which Columbus invoked so frequently, spoke of the sanctity of life and tried to save them. In fact, Friar Buil, head of the contingent of priests

Columbus being greeted by the Indians. An idealized interpretation by Théodore de Bry.

to come out later, equalled the soldiers in bloodthirstiness.

That tragedy still lay in the future. The remainder of the voyage of Columbus was more a light comedy, with the Spaniards wearily accepting the overwhelming hospitality and gifts of the population, but forever asking them with words and grunts and gestures where the gold was, and the palaces of the Grand Khan, and giving every island a new, Spanish, pious name.

The population were Arawak Indians, a people who had a

developed agriculture (corn, yams, cassava), who could spin and weave, but had no iron, no horses, no beasts of burden. The contemporary descriptions (tall, light brown, straight hair) gave them a physical type akin to the Polynesians of the Pacific Ocean. The best-known pictures show them that way, but most of these were drawn after pure Arawaks had vanished from the earth. Their society seems to have been based on village communes where most property was jointly held. They were ready to give everything they had to strangers, and they would take a while to learn that the Spaniards took, but put to death anyone who took from them.

Perhaps there is a danger of idealizing the life that these Indians led on what probably are still the most beautiful islands in the world. They certainly fought wars (as the Indians of the North American continent did) and had to defend themselves against raids by the Caribs, a different nation which maybe practiced cannibalism on its prisoners. But as every visitor, in those first days, describes with astonishment their friendliness, innocence, and high spirits, they clearly did live at peace with themselves and their environment.

Some of these people wore little gold ornaments in their ears or noses. Columbus had some of them captured and, with those ornaments as a reference, tried to have them guide him to the source of that gold. That way, he landed in Cuba on October 28, after zigzagging through the Bahamas. Cuba, he thought, must be Japan. "There," he wrote in his log, "I will speak with the King and see if I can get the gold that I hear he wears."

He sent a mission ashore to a place that was mentioned to him as Colbanacan (Colba was the Indian name for what is now Cuba), because he thought he recognized the name of the Grand Khan in that word—the ruler of China of two centuries earlier. Columbus, adding up the distance from his "real" log, thought he had sailed ninety degrees west from Palos (instead of less then seventy). Also, more surprisingly, he put his landing spot first at forty degrees north, then at thirty-four. He actually was just north of the twentieth degree. This is surprising because taking latitude is not that difficult an observation. But his talent lay in a feel for the wind and the water, not in mathematics.

From Cuba, Columbus, still piloted by his prisoners, sailed to what is now Haiti. There, fatally for its people, some little gold indeed used to be found in the rivers and was made by the Indians into tiny decorations. Columbus and his men were to latch on to this unhappy place like a vampire to its prey.

December 6, 1492, was the day on which Columbus made a landfall at a spot he called San Nicolas Môle. He continued sailing east, and named the island La Isla Española, for its supposed resemblance to Spain. It is unfortunately still called Hispaniola, embracing Haiti and the Dominican Republic. I say unfortunately, for there is something sinister in the fact that these places still bear the names given to them by their despoilers.

Columbus's own sketch of "la española," or northwest Hispaniola.

It was a combination of circumstances that made Hispaniola the first island to be doomed. There was the fact that the Pinta had sailed from Cuba to Haiti on her own. Martin Pinzón, who had taken his own batch of captives on Cuba, was told by them about gold fields on Haiti. Or better, that is what he wanted to hear and what he thought he heard them say. When he later caught up with, or was caught up by, Columbus in Haitian waters, he spilled the news as a token of his continued good will.

Another stroke of destiny was the Santa Maria foundering on a reef off the northwest point of the island. When he couldn't get her afloat, Columbus had the stores, and all wood that could be loosened, taken ashore, and decided to use it for building a fort right there.

A local chieftain or *cacique,* Guacanagari, had already met Columbus and sent him presents, including a gold mask which had heightened the Spaniard's gold fever. This cacique and his people now came out in all their canoes when they heard of the shipwreck, and they worked for hours to save the crew and the stores. These were placed on the beach, and Columbus expressed in his log everyone's surprise that "not a lace point" was stolen.

To me it is a measure of the man (whom I liked less, the more I read of and about him) that he now tried to convince the Indian chieftain that it was his fault that the ship, on its way to the alleged gold fields, had run aground. He conveyed to the cacique that he had been on his way to a return visit to his village, as he had been invited to do on the previous Saturday, "and because of that, I had lost my ship on a reef." "The King" (as Columbus called him) "wept . . . and sent me various of his relatives to implore me not to grieve, for he would give me everything he had."

The First Fort

The Santa Maria had been run aground on Christmas day, and the fort that Columbus built from its timbers was named Puerto de Navidad, Spanish for Christmas Harbor. It was the first European foothold in the Western Hemisphere (apart from a possible Viking settlement). Thirty-nine men eagerly volunteered to man it. They had the stores from the Santa Maria, and its boats, arms, and artillery, and got instuctions to collect as much gold as possible, and bury it under the settlement. As their commander, Columbus appointed one of the few men he trusted as a personal friend, Diego de Araña. Then he himself went over to the Niña.

Before setting sail, the Niña fired her lombard (a kind of mortar) at the hull of the Santa Maria on the reef and riddled it with cannon balls. This was done to impress the population, who fell to the ground at the noise, to the hilarity of the assembled Christians. It should have shown the Indians that their gentleness was not an accepted currency, but it didn't. The cacique Guacanagari gave a great farewell celebration before the Niña sailed.

The First Battle

All ships had already taken prisoners. That is to say, they had grabbed some of their visitors and locked them up, all "without noise or trouble," as Columbus' son Hernando put it in his later history of the voyages. The first open fight came before the Niña left Hispaniola, after she had met up again with the Pinta. The two ships had entered Samaná Bay near the eastern tip of the island, in what is now the Dominican Republic.

Here the local Indians had arms, bows of yew (like the English archers at the Battle of Agincourt), for here they were exposed to raiding Caribs from what is now Puerto Rico. Columbus had one of these Indians taken aboard, "his hair very long, in a net of parrot feathers, naked as the day he was born, speaking the proud language common to all peoples in this area" (to quote the story as written by Columbus' son). This man was then taken ashore, where he told his countrymen to lay down their arms.

Seven Spaniards now came ashore, and on Columbus' instructions tried to buy the bows and arrows with their hawks' bells and beads. The Indians traded them two bows but refused to sell more. After some shouting, the Spaniards set on them with their swords. They were seven against fifty, but they were also iron against flesh (and yew). Two Indians were quickly cut down, and the others fled, "surprised at our courage and the wounds made by our weapons," Hernando writes.

Then the Niña and the Pinta set course for Castile, to report on what they had found and done.

The Return Voyage

It took the Niña and Pinta a month, from mid-January to mid-February 1493, to get to the Azores. Their sailing luck was good, for as they tried to sail as close to the trade winds as possible, steering for Spain, they were, by the natural drift of a sailing vessel, driven ever farther north. That way, they reached thirty degrees north, and, as stated before, entered the region of the westerly winds. The caravels were leaking badly and the pumps had to be manned continuously.

When the ships caught the west wind, the weather turned cold, and the Indian prisoners began to die. Columbus and the pilots took a latitude observation which made them believe they were on the parallel of Cape St. Vincent in Portugal and they set a course due east. The compass variation probably sent them more northerly, east by north, and this happened to be precisely the route to get them to the Azores.

On February 14 they ran into a storm. They rightly guessed they were near the Azores, though they did not know how near. The very high winds shifted to the south, and the Pinta, less able to withstand the sea than the Niña, had to veer north. The ships were separated and did not meet again until they were in Palos harbor. The Pinta made a landfall in northern Spain, while the Niña, after an anxious night in which Columbus and his men made various vows to do penance if they were saved, sighted land: the little island of Santa Maria, the closest to Portugal of the Azores.

Santa Maria became the scene of a squabble. As part of the crew of the Niña trooped off to the nearest church to fulfill the vow made during the storm, the local Portuguese authorities put them in jail. They then sent a boat out to the Niña in a somewhat half-hearted attempt to arrest Columbus and the others too. Columbus held up the various letters and the passport he had carried to show the Grand Khan, and berated the Portuguese for being less hospitable than the heathens he had just visited. Presently, his credentials were accepted and the captured crewmen released.

That reception had had the officers of the Niña worried: they believed that war between Spain and Portugal might have broken out in their absence. This was not the case, but there was an awareness in Lisbon that its monopoly of the southern oceans was threatened. The captain of the Santa Maria garrison had suspected the Niña of having visited Africa, and Africa "belonged" to Portugal. Soon, this potential conflict would be settled in a summit conference which, with sublime simplicity, divided the world between Spain and Portugal.

The Niña sailed for Spain on February 24, through very high winds and seas. It couldn't round Cape St. Vincent, and so after some more pious vows by the crew, the ship safely sailed up the Tagus and anchored off Lisbon on March 4, 1493.

The Report by Columbus

While lying off the island of Santa Maria, Columbus wrote a report that was later sent out in several copies (presumably from Lisbon, and also from Palos) to persons at Court, and that was ultimately meant for the King and Queen. Most of the facts in it have already been mentioned, but it shows how Columbus wished them presented.

Here, as ever after, he would insist that he had reached Asia. And here, on the threshold of his great moment of triumph, he had already adopted that somewhat plaintive tone in which he would from then on, aggressively or defensively, boast of the importance of his discoveries.

It might have been assumed that Columbus could let his success speak for itself. But he did not want the fame of having found new lands; he wanted his islands to be the Asian nations of Marco Polo and Mandeville, with their gold-roofed palaces. Gold was his, and Spain's, obsession.

"As I know that you will be happy with the great success with which the Lord has crowned my voyage," his report starts out, "I write to tell you that I crossed in thirty-three days from the Canaries to the Indies. . . . I found very many islands and took possession of them all. No opposition was offered. . . .

"When I reached Cuba, I followed its north coast to the west, and found it so long that I felt this must be mainland, the province of Cathay [China]. . . . From there I saw another island eighteen leagues [about sixty miles] eastward which I named Hispaniola.

"Hispaniola is a miracle. Mountains and hills, plains and pastures, are both fertile and beautiful . . . the harbors are unbelievably good and there are many wide rivers of which the majority contain gold. . . . There are many spices, and great mines of gold and other metals. . . ." (All this, of course, was fantasy.)

"The inhabitants go naked . . . they have no iron or arms and are not capable of using them, not because they are not strong and well-built but because they are astonishingly shy. . . . We have not harmed any of them . . . true, when they have been reassured and lost their fear, they are so naive and so free with their possessions that no one who has not witnessed them would believe it. When you ask for something they have, they never say no. To the contrary, they offer to share with anyone. . . .

"I gave them a thousand pretty things in order to get their affection and make them want to become Christians. I hope to win them to the love and service of your Highnesses and of the Spanish nation, and make them collect and give us the things which they possess in abundance and which we need. . . . They believe that power and goodness are housed in the sky and they are absolutely convinced that I come from the sky with these ships and men. . . . They are men of great intelligence, for they navigate all their seas, and give an amazingly precise account of everything. . . .

"These islands are richer than I know or can say and I have taken possession of them in their Majesties' name and hold them all on their behalf, and as totally as the kingdom of Castile. In this island of Hispaniola I have taken possession of a large town, which is very well situated both for the gold fields and for communication with the mainland and the land of the Grand Khan, with whom there will be a very profitable commerce."

(This large town was actually the few huts on the spot where the Navidad fort was to be built; the "mainland" was Cuba, and the Grand Khan was out of the pages of Marco Polo.)

"I have established a warm friendship with the king of this land . . . but even should he change his attitude, the men I have left [at Navidad] would be enough to destroy the entire country." (This "king" was the local cacique Guacanagari.)

"As far as I could see, whatever a man has is shared among all, and this is especially true of food. I have not found the human monsters many expected. To the contrary, the whole population is well built. They are not Negroes as in Guinea, and their hair is straight. . . .

"In conclusion, to speak of the results of this very hasty voyage, their Majesties can see that I will give them as much gold as they need, if they will give me some very little help; and I will also give them all the spices and cotton they need, and as for resin [used in paint and varnish] which till now has only been found in Greece, and which the traders of Genoa sell at the price they choose, I will bring back as much of it as their

Majesties may order. . . . And I will bring back as much aloe [another resin], and as many slaves as they ask. . . . I think I have also found cinnamon. . . ." (All this, except for the slaves, was imaginary. The spiteful touch about Genoa is not without interest.)

"Thus the eternal God, Our Lord, gives victory to those who follow His way over apparent impossibilities. . . ."

And there follows a lengthy homily about how he had deserved the help of the Lord, and how all should rejoice at the pending conversion of so many people to "our Holy Faith." Here, as in the log, there are some words about those who didn't believe he could do it, and then mysteriously the letter signs off with the words, "Written in the caravel off the Canary Islands" (instead of the Azores). It is signed, as a reminder of a promise, "The Admiral."

The Reception

Columbus had been told to report to the master of the ship that guarded the port of Lisbon, but he refused, as he was now an admiral of the Crown of Castile, and he showed his various letters and papers instead. The news of his voyage caused a great sensation, and the following day so many people came to see the ship and the surviving Indians that (in the words of his son) "the sea could not be seen for all the Portuguese boats and sloops."

The day after, Columbus was summoned to the Court and was very well received by John II, the king who had once refused first chance to sponsor this expedition. Columbus was not above gloating, and it is amusing to think of the various

undercurrents during the politenesses exchanged. (It is, however, quite possible that if Columbus had sailed under the
Portuguese flag and had used the Azores instead of the Canaries as his staging port, he would not have made it.) King John
told Columbus that the places he had visited would go to
Portugal under the treaty he had made with Castile in 1479.
Columbus answered that he knew nothing about such a treaty;
all he could say was that he had not been in Africa. The matter
was left for others to negotiate.

On the way back to his ship, Columbus called on the
Queen, who was staying in a convent near Lisbon, and then
set sail for his port of departure, Palos, which he reached on
March 14, seven months and eleven days after sailing.

The Pinta came into port just after him. Her captain, Martin
Pinzón, had already sent word about the expedition to the
King and Queen in Barcelona from his first port of landing,
Bayona. But he had been told not to come to the Court
without his commander Columbus. He was a sick man and
probably also furious and disappointed by his failure to be
there first. He sailed to Palos, went home, and died a few
weeks later.

As for Columbus, he travelled in triumph from Palos first
to Seville, where he received a royal letter addressed to "Don
Cristóbal Colón, Admiral of the Ocean Sea, Viceroy and
Governor of the islands he has discovered in the Indies." Thus
he found the promises of the Capitulations confirmed. He
then went on in state to the Court in Barcelona, his report
ready on how Hispaniola should be colonized.

With him came some of his ship's officers, the last six
surviving Indians, and servants hired for the occasion. Wherever the company passed, the natives flocked to the road to
gape, for in spite of the chilly spring of Castile, the Indians had

to walk in their natural clothing, that is, nothing but feathers and a little apron for modesty's sake. Thus they entered Barcelona on April 20, where the entire Court and city came out to watch.

Columbus had all the honor he could have dreamed of: the King and Queen allowed him to sit down in their presence with his hat on (a privilege only some grandees of Spain shared), and when the King rode out, the Infante Don Juan rode on one side and the Admiral on the other.

Tordesillas

A second voyage was immediately prepared, but first there was King John's assertion, that those newly seen islands were his, to clear up. To Spain and Portugal, no other nation at that time counted, and they blithely met, with the Pope as arbiter, to divide the rest of the world between them. Legally (in medieval Church terms), all newly discovered land "belonged" to the Pope and was his to give in fief to those kings who would then have the duty to lead the inhabitants to the True Faith. It is worth noting about this division of the world that no one seemed to worry about the eventual reaction of the Emperor of Japan or that of the Grand Khan, who was supposedly ruling China.

Pope Alexander VI "most liberally" (again, in the words of Columbus' son Hernando) granted the "Catholic Sovereigns Ferdinand and Isabella all they had conquered so far and also everything they would still discover farther west as far as the Orient, and forbade all others to encroach on these boundaries." Pope Alexander was one of the famous, or infamous,

Borgias of Spanish birth, and he was a protégé of Ferdinand and Isabella. During the year 1493, he issued a series of papal bulls outlining his thoughts on the subject, and in May he finally set the line west of which everything would go to Spain, at one hundred leagues (about four hundred land miles) west of the Azores. Such a line ran roughly thirty-five degrees west, and Portugal was not satisfied with it, although it stayed well west of Africa.

In 1494, Spain and Portugal reopened direct negotiations and reached an agreement in the town of Tordesillas in central Spain, endorsed by Pope Alexander. At Tordesillas, the line was moved to 370 leagues, or 1,400 miles, west of the Cape Verde Islands. That moved the Portuguese share of the world near the fifty degree west meridian and "gave" it a solid chunk of Brazil and the Newfoundland banks; but the problem of determining longitude still caused numerous local adjustments afterward.

The inhabitants of those unhappy "new" countries had no power to resist, but the other nations of Europe did. The King of France said, "Where is it written that the world is already divided up?" French fishermen went to Newfoundland without worrying about the Pope, while Holland occupied most of Brazil for a time.

But for centuries afterward, Spain used the Treaty of Tordesillas as a basis for the garrotting (strangling to death with a cord and stick) of foreign sailors caught in their half of the world.

At the time of the Pope's confirmation of the sovereignty of Spain over the "Indies," the sovereigns confirmed Columbus' governorship once more and appointed him captain-general of the second voyage he was to undertake. They also gave him a coat of arms, with a castle and a lion. Because of their connotation with the names of the Spanish kingdoms, Castile and León, those emblems were most coveted by Spanish gentlemen.

5

THE SECOND VOYAGE

There is no ship's log in existence for the second voyage of Columbus to America, but there is much material, and foremost among it the report by Diego Chanca. Chanca was one of the Court physicians, and the King and Queen sent him on the expedition and paid his salary. He didn't stay with Columbus but went back to Spain on the first ship returning.

Geographically no other crossing, obviously, matched the first one. The mystery barrier had been broken. Henceforth, ships from many countries would sail west. Before the century had ended, Europeans would have set foot on American soil from Newfoundland (John Cabot) to Brazil. In the words of a writer of the period, "the works of Creation were doubled."

But for the native population of America, the second Columbus voyage was perhaps the crucial one. On that occasion, the pattern was set for centuries to come. The pretense was ended, the idyll over. The Indians, who had been praised for their generosity and innocence, were now called savages. The talk was of slavery and gold, rather than of brotherhood and conversion. The new relationship between the races was established.

I am not going to assert that this was all Columbus' fault. Although there was no systematic slavery within Europe at that time, enslavement of darker races had been considered a matter of course from the first contact with them. The Portuguese were buying slaves on the Guinea coast, though not catching them themselves—a moot distinction.

Dangerous as such generalizations are, a case can be made that the Spaniards from that time on became more cruel than any of the other seagoing nations of Europe—more cruel toward their own poor as well. Soon they would be treating the Indians, in the words of Bishop de las Casas, "not as beasts, for beasts are treated properly at times, but like the excrement in a public square." De las Casas, who was an admirer, not an enemy, of Columbus, said that Columbus was "at the beginning of the ill usage inflicted upon them." (But then, when we think of children pulling coal wagons in British mines—not in 1492 but in 1852—even this ill usage becomes relative.)

This is not to say that the picture of Spain in America is totally black. There were forces for the good besides Bishop de las Casas. Columbus assuredly was not a force for the good. If an entire race stood in his way, it had to go.

Surprisingly, Ferdinand and Isabella, the sovereigns who had instituted the dreaded Inquisition in 1480 and expelled all Jews in 1492, seemed a force of moderation. Their express command to the Admiral for his second voyage was that the Indians were to be treated "well and lovingly."

It was a half-hearted command, however. These two, who always called themselves "the Catholic Monarchs," appear not to have taken any specific steps when the various priests who went and returned did not convert one single Indian, and when instead the ships started returning with enslaved men, women and children.

Only when the slave trade had stopped making profits for the Crown or anyone else, because the Arawaks could not survive under its conditions, did the Crown terminate the practice. By then, the Arawak nation was already doomed.

Unfortunately, this is not the only instance in Western history where men became humane at the very moment inhumanity lost its business advantage.

The Crossing

The report by Columbus about the first voyage—his sales prospectus, so to speak—saw to it that this time there was no shortage of candidates for the Enterprise. No less than seventeen ships set out, with twelve to fifteen hundred men. Many others wanted to go and were refused. The organization of the expedition, for that time enormous, was not left to Columbus, but was carried out by Juan de Fonseca, archdeacon of Seville, who would henceforth continue to act as a quartermaster-general for the American sailings.

Another "Santa Maria" was the flagship for this fleet; most of the other ships' names are not known. Some were very small, and meant for inshore exploration. (Twelve of them were to turn around upon reaching the New World.) The Niña went again, and some members of the Niño family who owned her. The Pinzóns did not go; they were no longer on speaking terms with Columbus. Two hundred passengers, gentleman adventurers, were going at their own expense.

This fleet sailed on September 25, 1493, from Cádiz, which is some sixty miles down the coast from Palos. Again, the Canary Islands were the first port of call, and they sailed from there on October 13. Three weeks later, on November 3, they sighted land: the island Dominica in the Lesser Antilles.

The ease of this passage makes you wonder again for a moment why it had not been done long before. The answer is, indeed, illustrated by the story of Columbus making his egg stand on end: once you know how, it's simple. This is especially true with the westward voyages, which, different from the Portuguese endeavors around Africa, led through blessed climates and seas that were tempestuous only on rare occasions. The hardships of these crossings at no time took the terrifying toll of the tropical voyages.

From Dominica, the fleet went island-hopping, sailing north, past (what are now called) Guadeloupe, Montserrat, the Virgin Islands, Puerto Rico, and finally on to their principal destination, Hispaniola.

They staged brief reconnaissances on most islands. Dr. Chanca comments on their lushness, even at that time of year, the green shores, or then again mountains rising from the sea with waterfalls of dizzying height. Chanca reports that everywhere captives were taken, but he also notes that a number of Indians came freely aboard the ships. These had been captives themselves of raiding Caribs. In most places, the men were away on fishing expeditions and the women and children who could, fled. Different from the experience of the first voyage, here most villages stood empty when the Spaniards came ashore.

Their first meeting with Indians who tried to defend themselves came in mid-November, off a small island, probably Saint Martin (Sint Maarten).

The Admiral was lying offshore and a boat he had sent out was on its way back with captives. Then, as related by Chanca, a canoe appeared around the point of land with four men, two women, and a child. When they saw the Spanish fleet, they were so astounded that, in the words of Chanca, "they remained without a motion, a whole hour, at about a reach of two mortar shots from the ships."

It is a particularly clear and haunting image for me: that motionless canoe, with its seven people, just sitting and staring at the seventeen ships reflected in the blue water, under a blue sky.

But to the Spaniards these people were game rather than fellow beings.

Several boats set out to get them, hugging the shore and unseen by the Indians, who were "lost in amazement." At the last moment, the Indians saw their attackers approach, and when they realized they could not get away, they took up their bows, men and women alike, to defend themselves, first from their canoe and then, when that had been upturned, standing in the shallow water.

They were overpowered and brought to the Santa Maria. One, whose stomach had been slit open by a Spaniard, was tossed overboard, but he swam toward shore, holding his guts in with his hand. The gallant Spaniards went after him, captured him anew, and this time threw him overboard after binding his hands and feet. The Indian managed to free himself, and swam off once more. Then he was "shot through and through" from the deck of the ship and sank in the clear water.

This happened during what Columbus' American biographer Samuel Eliot Morison calls "those bright November days, the fleet gaily coasting, . . .and hearty voices joining in the evening hymn to the Blessed Virgin."

Hispaniola Revisited

As Columbus was approaching Hispaniola from the east on this occasion, none of his old crew recognized it; the captive Indians told them where they were. Presently they saw the Bay of Samaná, and from then on they followed the north coast which was familiar to them, on to Fort Navidad.

Toward the end of November, late in the evening, Columbus reached the place. Remembering the wreck of his first Santa Maria, he stayed offshore and had a cannon fired. But no answer came from the fort.

In the night a canoe of Indians approached, men from the villages of Guacanagari. They brought presents and told him all was well; but their fearfulness showed it was not.

Soon the Admiral learned through his two interpreters—survivors from the captives of the first voyage—that all inhabitants of his first colony had been killed. They had roamed the island in gangs, looking for more gold than even the ever willing Guacanagari could find for them, and taking any woman or boy they fancied. Other caciques were less fearful than Guacanagari, and finally the misdeeds of the Spaniards became so unbearable that those "gentle, timid souls" rose against them and killed them in a pitched battle. They then marched on Navidad where they found only ten Spanish settlers who had stayed home, each with a bevy of enslaved girls, and these were overpowered and killed too.

Through it all, Guacanagari had remained in his role of the friend of Columbus and had tried to prevent this revenge.

The evil deeds committed by the Spanish colonists must indeed have been staggering, for that first day the Admiral and his officers did not speak of retaliation—and that at a time when an Indian already had his ears cut off if he touched a Spanish article of clothing. Only Friar Buil, head of the priests who had come to convert the savages to Christian love, wanted Guacanagari put to death "as an example." Columbus decided to wait and see. Guacanagari was his ally, his only one.

The Admiral immediately ordered the ground of Navidad turned over with spades. Gold was still and always his first thought, and before sailing, he had given orders to those men to bury all the gold they got on the spot. It is not known if anything was found beyond the buried bodies of the Spaniards.

The Admiral then decided to set up a new settlement and had the surrounding area reconnoitered. After their experience with the Navidad men, the Indian mood was very different. No more jubilation; whenever the Spaniards reached a village, they found that all the inhabitants had fled.

Ten women, whom Columbus had captured earlier, jumped overboard and tried to escape. Four were caught with the boats as they came out of the water, but the others made it inland. Guacanagari must have been more and more uncomfortable in what had become a role of traitor to his people, for Columbus now sent him a messenger, demanding that he find the six women and return them to the ships. (They were to be used as sex slaves for the crew.)

Against hard eastern winds and much rain, the entire fleet then proceeded along the coast, looking for a new place for a fort. They were steering in the direction of the alleged gold fields of Cibao in central Hispaniola that Pinzón had reported on the first voyage. On January 2, 1494, they anchored in a sheltered bay and started building a new fort, which they called Isabela (with one *l,* after the Spanish "Isabel" of the Queen's name).

By now, according to Dr. Chanca, a third of the men had fallen sick. Although he ascribed this to the air, the water, the climate, and the general "beastliness" of the place, there was another and quite different reason, as we will see later. Apart from all the sickness, the work involved in building the fort, and the difference between reality and the picture painted by Columbus in his report, made for much resentment among the expedition. After only a few days at Isabela, Columbus decided to send a large contingent home, together with what he thought was sandalwood and pepper (it wasn't), twenty-six captured Indians, and all the gold they had scraped together from the Indians in that short time. Twelve of the seventeen ships were sent right back after a rather useless voyage, and on one of them went Dr. Chanca.

Just before Chanca left, two reconnaissance parties sent out by Columbus had returned with reports of gold fields with riches beyond even Spanish greed. Chanca didn't question the finds. He ends his chronicle by assuring his readers that "the King and Queen will henceforth be the richest and most prosperous in the world, for nothing comparable has ever been seen or read of in the whole creation. . . . On the next voyage the ships will carry away such quantities of gold that anyone who hears of it will be dumbfounded."

From Isabela, Columbus promptly mounted a number of expeditions into the interior. He himself led the first one. Armored and helmeted, with swords and muskets, horses and fierce dogs, the Spaniards marched through the green valleys and up the hills of the island, banners flying and trumpets sounding. It was a most inconvenient and sweaty way of traveling in that humid climate, but the idea was that a show of force would stamp out any nonsensical ideas the natives might have begun to harbor. The target of these marches was of course those gold fields in Cibao, fields "as large as Portugal" in the words of Columbus' son. He, many years later, still clung to Columbus' fantasies—fantasies fatal to the island.

In reality, there were no gold fields anywhere, just a few rivers carrying grains of gold in alluvial form.

Columbus gave orders to build a fort near those nonexistent gold mines, and he named it San Tomas, presumably because of the Doubting Thomases among those adventurers in his train who still didn't believe in the promised riches. He put all the weapons in Isabela aboard his flagship because he was afraid of trouble from his colleagues. He then placed the settlement under the command of his young brother, Diego, the only man he now trusted, and set off himself for a reconnaissance of China—that is to say, Cuba.

Cuba and Jamaica

In April, Columbus, with two other ships, crossed from Hispaniola to Cuba, which he once more took "possession" of by planting a cross. Then he and his officers decided to follow the southern coastline. According to Aristotle, it is in the south rather than the north that all good things (gold and spices, that is) are found. From the south coast, they sailed to Jamaica, two days' sailing farther south. For Jamaica was called "Jamesque" by its inhabitants, and that name sounded to the Spaniards like "Babeque," another mystic place reputed to be crammed full of (even greed gets monotonous) . . . gold.

But nothing was found but Indians less friendly than the Arawaks had once been. However, they were soon taught to obey or flee, after crossbowmen from the ships had killed some of them and others had been savaged by the dogs the Spaniards had brought. This particular stratagem had first been used by Spain against the original inhabitants (long since exterminated) of the Canary Islands. Trained dogs are a terrible weapon against unarmed and naked men and women, and the Spaniards (like their French successors on Hispaniola) exulted in the results. South Africa's police dogs have a long history.

Columbus followed the Jamaican shore for a short while and then sailed back up to the southern coast of Cuba. He followed it to the gulf due south of where Havana now is. There, plagued by contrary winds and disease, he decided to return to Isabela.

In 1488, Bartolomeu Diaz had rounded the Cape of Good Hope and had been well on his way to India when his crew refused to continue. Diaz had returned to Lisbon, but first he had every man sign a deposition that Africa had indeed been rounded and the way east found. With this as a supposed example, Columbus now had every man on his ships, under threat of dire punishment, sign a deposition saying (what no one knew) that there was no need to go any farther west, as the length of their voyage had proven Cuba not to be an island— no island could be that long—but the mainland of Asia!

Once more, the Admiral acted as if saying or writing something with enough emphasis made it so. In doing that, he might look like the first public relations man, a worthy, if somewhat pathetic, predecessor of New York City's Madison

Avenue. But what moved Columbus was deeper, and more frightening. He seemed to be accumulating within himself that terrible ire of a man who feels that he alone is right, and that the world is forever conspiring against him, and not giving him his due.

It was a tough voyage back, which led the fleet once more to Jamaica and all around it this time, to dodge unfavorable winds.

From Jamaica they crossed to the southern shore of Hispaniola and followed the coastline. When they had made it to the southeastern tip of the island, they were lucky enough to witness a total eclipse of the moon. This, with the help of an astronomical table, gave them the time difference between their point of observation and the place for which the eclipse table was drawn, Nuremberg.

This was indeed luck, for such an event was the only way then to find longitude. It was a simple method: one hour's difference in time meant fifteen degrees longitude. The only error would be in measuring the time span from the observation to noon of the following day, in order to get local time. Columbus should have found that he was about five hours and twenty minutes behind Nuremberg, that is, almost eighty degrees west of it. But wittingly or unwittingly his sum came out at 103 degrees west of that town. Thus, he could tell himself once more that he had indeed just been to the Asian shores.

Shortly thereafter, the three ships rounded the eastern tip of the island, and toward the end of September Columbus landed once more at Isabela. He had been away more than half a year.

6

A NEW WORLD

Columbus' brother Diego had been in charge of Isabela in his absence. The gold collecting had been entrusted by him to two men, conquistadores, captains, robber barons, bandits: the proper name depends on your point of view. They were Pedro Margarit and Alonso de Hojeda.

Catholic Europe in those days was ready to call non-Christians "idolaters," worshippers of idols; that label was a sentence to death or to slavery. Hojeda himself was precisely what should be called an idolater, for he had a medal with the Virgin Mary on it around his neck and so steadfastly believed it made him invulnerable that he performed deeds of incredible daring, and cruelty. He and Margarit ransacked the Vega Real for six months, stealing the gold and the food while enslaving boys and taking girls for concubines. The Vega Real, or Royal Meadow, was a long central valley of Haiti and it had received that name from Columbus in order to give thanks (in the words of de las Casas) to God for its beauty, "for the Admiral was deeply moved by such things."

That emotion had not saved the valley from destruction. In the Admiral's absence, his brother Bartolomé had also shown up at Isabela. He had returned to Spain from his efforts to enlist the kings of England or France in the Enterprise, to learn that his brother had already found "the Indies" and gone back there a second time. He hastened to follow him; three caravels, with provisions for the island, were provided by the Spanish monarchs. The Admiral thus found another ally he trusted upon his return, and he promptly made his brother *adelantado*— governor—of the Indies.

But Pedro Margarit used one of Bartolomé's ships to leave the island and go back to Spain. He had refused to recognize the authority of either Diego or Bartolomé and had announced he could no longer stomach or condone the treatment meted out to the Indians. Another man who decided he had had enough was Friar Buil, the priest who had asked for the death of Guacanagari. These, and others who joined them later, began lobbying at Court against Columbus, demanding that he return. Hispaniola, they said, was in chaos. Hojeda had not joined these dissidents and stayed on.

The Columbus brothers now set out to extend their dominion over the entire island and to see to the "pacification" of the Indians. This word had become familiar to us from the Vietnam War, and was already in use then with the same hidden meaning. The reason that the inhabitants of the island, whose almost unbelievable peacefulness and hospitality had been described so eloquently by the Admiral himself, now needed "pacifying," was obvious. The rampaging of Margarit and Hojeda had stirred even these gentle tribes into resistance.

The Admiral, far from aiming at healing those terrible wrongs, made them into a system. He was determined to somehow squeeze the fabulous wealth that he had announced, but that wasn't there, out of this poor island. He saw two ways: gold and slaves.

We are now in February 1495. Time was short for sending back a good "dividend" on the supply ships getting ready for the return to Spain. Columbus therefore turned to a massive slave raid as a means for filling up these ships. The brothers rounded up fifteen hundred Arawaks—men, women, and children—and imprisoned them in pens in Isabela, guarded by men and dogs. The ships had room for no more than five hundred, and thus only the best specimens were loaded aboard. The Admiral then told the Spaniards they could help themselves from the remainder to as many slaves as they wanted. Those whom no one chose were simply kicked out of their pens. Such had been the terror of these prisoners that (in the description by Michele de Cuneo, one of the colonists) "they rushed in all directions like lunatics, women dropping and abandoning infants in the rush, running for miles without stopping, fleeing across mountains and rivers."

Of the five hundred slaves, three hundred arrived alive in Spain, where they were put up for sale in Seville by Don Juan de Fonseca, the archdeacon of the town. "As naked as the day they were born," the report of this excellent churchman says, *"but with no more embarrassment than animals."*

(When the first photographs of the victims of the Mylai massacre in Vietnam were published in the United States, there was much protest against the fact that you could see the bare behinds and the penises of the corpses.)

The slave trade immediately turned out to be "unprofitable, for the slaves mostly died." Columbus decided to concentrate on gold, although he writes, "Let us *in the name of the Holy Trinity* go on sending all the slaves that can be sold."

There now began a reign of terror on Hispaniola for which I

can find no proper historical parallel. Our world has a long and cruel history, and the word "unprecedented" should perhaps not ever be used. But the unique horror of Columbus' new state was that even the blindest obedience could not save the people. What was demanded of them was the impossible. Here was indeed created a new and unheard of society.

Death of a Nation

To fill the empty ships going back to Castile, to stop his detractors from talking, to prove his success, Columbus needed gold. And the following system was adopted for this end.

Every man and woman, every boy or girl of fourteen or older, in the province of Cibao (of the imaginary gold fields) had to collect gold for the Spaniards. As their measure, the Spaniards used those same miserable hawks' bells, the little trinkets they had given away so freely when they first came "as if from Heaven." Every three months, every Indian had to bring to one of the forts a hawks' bell filled with gold dust. The chiefs had to bring in about ten times that amount. In the other provinces of Hispaniola, twenty-five pounds of spun cotton took the place of gold.

Copper tokens were manufactured, and when an Indian had brought his or her tribute to an armed post, he or she received such a token, stamped with the month, to be hung around the neck. With that they were safe for another three months while collecting more gold.

Whoever was caught without a token was killed by having his or her hands cut off. There are old Spanish prints (I saw them in the collection of Bishop Voegeli of Haiti) that show this being done: the Indians stumble away, staring *with surprise* at their arm stumps pulsing out blood.

There were no gold fields, and thus, once the Indians had handed in whatever they still had in gold ornaments, their only hope was to work all day in the streams, washing out gold dust from the pebbles. It was an impossible task, but those Indians who tried to flee into the mountains were systematically hunted down with dogs and killed, to set an example for the others to keep trying.

By that time there was no longer a possibility of mass resistance. The Admiral, his brother Bartolomé, and Hojeda had crushingly defeated the only army the Indians ever managed to bring together. Armor, muskets, swords, horses, and dogs had made the Spaniards invincible. All prisoners had been hanged or burned to death. The island was so well pacified that a Spaniard could go anywhere, take any woman or girl, take anything, and have the Indians carry him on their backs as if they were mules.

Thus it was at this time that the mass suicides began: the Arawaks killed themselves with cassava poison.

During those two years of the administration of the brothers Columbus, an estimated one half of the entire population of Hispaniola was killed or killed themselves. The estimates run from 125,000 to one-half million.

Then, in 1496, when there was obviously not one grain of gold left, the gold tribute system was changed to that of the *repartimientos,* later known as the *encomiendas.* The Spaniards cut out estates for themselves; the Indians still living on this land became their property. They could be used to work the land for the owner or could be hired out indefinitely as labor gangs anywhere else. These gangs "were marched all over the

Indians having their hands chopped off for failing to meet the gold dust quota.
From a book by Bartolomé de las Casas entitled Spanish Cruelties,
published in 1609.

island, from one end to the other." The same setup was later
introduced in all the new Spanish possessions in the Americas.

The killings continued at no less speed. In 1515 there were
not more than ten thousand Indians left alive; twenty-five
years later, the entire nation had vanished from the earth. Not
one Indian on the island had ever been converted to what
Columbus called "our Holy Faith."

The hardier black slaves from Africa were brought in to
take their place. They would, at the end of the eighteenth
century, stage the first and perhaps only successful slave revolt

The Spaniards hanging Indians and setting fire to their houses. Engraving from Bartolomé de las Casas.

in Western history. It made Haiti, the western half of the island, the second independent republic of this hemisphere.

The death toll among the blacks had been frightful too, but they had been brought in such numbers that enough of them survived to form a nation. The statistics (not very precise, obviously) in the archives of Port-au-Prince (now Haiti's capital) show that two million slaves were imported in the century before independence. Of these, and all their children, six hundred thousand survived when their revolution began.

Columbus' Enterprise, by the Year 1496

In October 1495, the anti-Columbus lobby in Spain had succeeded in making the Court nervous. The monarchs sent out an investigator to report directly to them on the state of Hispaniola. His arrival made the Admiral decide to go back to Spain and defend his record. In March 1496, he left Isabela aboard the Niña, accompanied by a small ship built from the timbers of various shipwrecks.

By then, the number of Spanish colonists on the island was about six hundred. They were constantly clamoring for fresh supplies from Spain, for in spite of the abundance of fertile land, now virtually uninhabited, and the slaves still available, they were unable to become self-sufficient. There was also an increasing number who were very sick. Both these aspects of the Enterprise need some further comment.

From the very first, the Spaniards did not come to the Indies (the Americas, that is) to settle. They came to trade, or to put it less hypocritically, to plunder, and then to return home to Castile with the loot. They were, from the very first, mentally at war with their surroundings. This, certainly, was one reason why in these islands, blessed by nature, they acted, and reported home, as if they were in some barren wasteland, unable to raise any food of their own, unable to use the abundance of fish and fowl even to stay alive.

An added handicap was the contempt any Spaniard with two pesos to rub together nursed against manual labor. There was a later voyage when Columbus and his "gentleman travelers" (*hidalgos*) stayed marooned for months on end on a wild coast rather than pull themselves together and build a little boat. If you compare their helplessness with the self-reliance of, for instance, the French fishermen and the English

fur-traders in the North, the difference is almost too enormous to understand. But this hard hatred, or at best disdain,
for their surroundings, this *gangster* mentality of the Spanish
conquistadores, goes part way to explain their inhumanity,
both toward the inhabitants of the lands they conquered and
toward each other.

Another peculiarity of the Enterprise by now was the
spread of disease. A new disease had appeared, first among the
colonists, then, brought home by them, in Spain, Italy, and
France, and from there spreading through Europe. It was a
disease until recently incurable, and perhaps more feared than
any other: syphilis, or as it was then called in English, the great
pox (as compared to the relatively less terrible smallpox).
After their own destruction, the Indians of the Caribbean
brought a strange, if to them useless, revenge upon their
destroyers through syphilis.

Syphilis seems to have been an endemic, nonfatal and
almost symptomless affliction among the Indians of the Caribbean and South America. Traces of the spirillum (bacteria)
of the disease, *Treponema pallidum,* have been found in the
bones of pre-Columbian Indians. But once caught by Europeans, the disease flared up in a totally different form, virulent
and lethal.

Syphilis—until the days of antibiotics—could, in the classic
medical school phrase, "do anything, and look like anything."
It was called "the great imitator." Its final chapter was usually
death, through the destruction of the nervous system or other
physical deterioration. Syphilis is transmitted only in sexual
contact, and it was the just price the Spaniards paid for their
ravaging of the Indian women. Of course, from that time on
many thousands of innocent lives continued to pay this price.

Some Columbus fans (the foremost of whom is S.E. Morison)

don't deny that the Spaniards raped the Indian women, but like to wrap it in a kind of boys-will-be-boys chuckle. To get away from the curse of syphilis, they have come forward with the thesis that the disease was not brought back to Europe by the thousands of Spaniards who had caught it in America, but, of all people, by the six shivering Indians who had survived Columbus' kidnapping. These poor devils (the survivors of whom were actually taken back by Columbus as interpreters), so this theory goes, infected the women in the brothels of Barcelona, and that is where it all started. The evil is more

Columbus and his men industriously rebuilding their ship. This engraving, by Théodore de Bry, seems far removed from what actually happened.

easily understood that way. You see, then it stems from lustful savages taking their pleasure with white women. (Morison, for one, announces that "medical authorities" have assured him the Niña crew couldn't have worked the ship on its way home if they had had syphilis; it had to be the Indians who were sick. As any first-year medical student knows, though, syphilis, "which can do anything," often does not noticeably affect a person's health for periods of as much as two years or more after infection.)

But in more recent studies of the subject, it is suggested that in fact the Indians' revenge was a feeble one. Syphilis, it is now often believed, already existed in Europe, but only after the epidemic upsurge of its American variant was it recognized as a venereal disease. Pre-Columbian syphilis in Europe had been confused with leprosy, according to this theory.

The syphilitic, grumbling, unhappy colony left behind by Columbus in March 1496 knew that nothing much further could be squeezed out of that cursed spot. Brother Bartolomé, left behind in command, started shifting the settlement to the southern coast, where a new town was started, Santo Domingo. The Spaniards there and at home began to look farther afield, and soon the importance of these "golden isles" was simply as a springboard for the conquest of Central and South America. There, in later years, more gold and silver would be found— indeed, the shiploads Columbus had dreamed of. And more terrible cruelties would be committed.

The Caribbean islands led Spain on to Mexico, Peru, and the Pacific. For one thing Columbus had doubtless achieved: the Atlantic had lost its terror. The crossings, just four years after that first voyage, were already becoming routine.

Columbus was on his way home, that spring of 1496, to defend his regime in Hispaniola and to try to get support for yet another expedition to locate the elusive Grand Khan of China. It took the Niña and her companion caravel, sailing by way of Guadeloupe, six weeks to reach Cádiz, in one of the Admiral's toughest voyages. Rations were so short that the crew repeatedly suggested eating the Indian slaves on the ship or at least throwing them overboard. Before it came to that, they sighted the Portuguese coast. Presently the two ships entered the Bay of Cádiz they had left almost three years earlier.

In one of his reports to his sovereigns, Columbus later summed up his second voyage in one paragraph: ". . .by the Grace of God, I discovered in a very brief time fifteen hundred miles of mainland, the end of the East . . . [in reality, Cuba] seven hundred important islands in addition to those discovered on my first voyage, and I sailed around the island of Hispaniola, which is greater in circumference than all of Spain [it isn't], and has a vast population, all of whom must pay tribute."

That was the voyage that sealed the fate of an island, and of generations of Indians born and yet unborn.

7

THE THIRD VOYAGE

The attitude of the Catholic monarchs toward Columbus at this point was not the "incredible ingratitude" of the Columbus myth, but simply a disappointment with the achievements he himself had aimed for: he had not asked for acclaim as a discoverer, but had presented himself as an entrepreneur announcing unheard-of mountains of gold.

He was kept cooling his heels in Cádiz and later in Seville for several months. He dressed as a friar and lived in the house of a priest, maybe to show his humility. Finally he was invited to the Court, then assembled at Valladolid (or, perhaps, Burgos) in northwestern Spain. Once again he set out, with servants carrying parrots and his Indians dressed only in feathers and gold ornaments (theirs to wear just for the trip). It was not the triumph of the first time, but his rank was once more confirmed. His two sons (one from his marriage, another born later) were pages at the Court. He had definitely escaped his origins. His request for ships to go on a new expedition met with only a lukewarm response, though. Some ships with supplies and colonists, including the first women, were sent to

Hispaniola in 1497, but Columbus himself did not sail again until May 1498.

A fleet of six vessels was assembled for him. Part of the money had been raised from a sale of enslaved Indians brought back by one of the Niño brothers: that helped. Also, royal worry about what the Portuguese might be up to must have helped overcome the lack of enthusiasm at Court. In fact, at the very time Columbus sailed from Seville, Vasco da Gama arrived in Calicut on the coast of India, at the end of the first sea passage.

Three ships of this, the third Columbus expedition, were sent straight to Hispaniola. The other three, with Columbus in command, went once more after Cathay. In order to gain the latitude he wanted, the Admiral this time sailed from the Canaries on south, along the route the Portuguese took to the Cape. At a latitude of about nine degrees north Columbus set a western course. (He had left the Cape Verde Islands behind, and actually thought he was at five degrees north.) In summer, the doldrums reach north of ten degrees latitude, and the fleet was becalmed for a very hot and miserable period. But the sea luck of Columbus held, and presently the ships caught a northeasterly wind. After a very rapid crossing, they sighted land. It was an island, and it was named Trinidad.

Here they took on fresh water and continued along the south shore of the island. After a short foray into the Gulf of Paria, between the island and the mainland, they rounded the mainland through the narrow passage that separates it from Trinidad and proceeded west, following the coastline of South America. When they reached the island of Margarita, Columbus set a very precise course for a return to Hispaniola across the Caribbean Sea.

As he had become convinced that the coast he had followed

up to Margarita was not an island but the long-coveted mainland, it is not clear why Columbus did not persist longer, but steered north (or rather, northwest by north) after only two hundred miles. Among the reasons given by himself, and later by his son Hernando, were the fact that the supplies he carried for Hispaniola began to spoil, his state of health (arthritis, eye trouble), and his nervousness at what seemed to him the erratic behavior of his compass needle.

Thus, he ended his exploration of the South American mainland coastline after six weeks, though he would return to it once more on his fourth and last voyage.

Paradise Found

I will not try to analyze the psychology of the report of this reconnaisance that Columbus sent to his monarchs. The voyage from Trinidad, past the western corner of the delta of the great Orinoco River, and then on to Margarita Island, became in his writing nothing less than the discovery of the Garden of Eden.

"I have always read that the world of land and sea is round," Columbus wrote in his dispatch to Spain, sent from Hispaniola, "but now I have found such irregularities that I have come to the following conclusion: it is not round but has the shape of a pear,. . .or like a woman's breast with a nipple . . . its point, nearest to the sky, lies below the equator . . . at the farthest point to the east, where all land and islands end.

"This belief is supported by what happened on crossing a line four hundred and fifty miles west of the Azores. [That is, about thirty-five degrees west.] As we passed it, going west, the ships rose gently nearer the sky, and the weather was mild. Because of this, the compass needle shifted by a quarter north-westward, and went on farther west as we proceeded. It is this increase in height that changes the circle made by the Pole Star. . . ." (Thus Columbus partially accounted for some very rough and mistaken observations he had made of that star.)

"I do not in the least question the roundness of that [Eastern] Hemisphere, but the other hemisphere resembles the half of a round pear with a raised stalk. . . . On passing the line of which I have spoken, I found the temperatures growing softer [i.e., less hot], and when I came to Trinidad, where the Pole Star also stands at five degrees at nightfall [that is, as at Sierra Leone; actually Trinidad is ten degrees north], the inhabitants were lighter and fairer [than the Africans]. . . . All this is to be attributed to the gentle climate, and this in turn to the fact that this land is highest on the surface of the world, nearest to the sky."

After quoting Aristotle on the "smallness of the earth," he went on to say, "I think the earthly Paradise lies here, which no one can enter but by God's permission." The Garden of Eden, Columbus wrote, must lie at the very point of this nipple, the height of which makes the climate cool and delicious. Only that can explain the strength of the currents in the Gulf of Paria, and the fresh-water currents sweeping out into it (from the Orinoco River). For in the medieval tradition, the four great rivers of the world, the Ganges, the Nile, the Tigris, and the Euphrates, all spring from a well in the Garden of Eden. Here, then, was the mouth of the Ganges.

Columbus continued this argument at great length, quoting Pliny, Nicolas of Lyra, his old bedtime author Pierre d'Ailly,

Seneca, and the Prophet Esdras from the apocryphal books of the Bible.

From this paradisical vision, Columbus' report proceeded, "May it please God to forgive those who have libeled and who libel this noble Enterprise and who oppose it. . . ." He reminds the monarchs of how little money all this has cost, relatively, and how long the princes of Portugal have persisted in their efforts. He tells them they now have "another world" in which the Holy Faith can be extended ("I tell all the people here of the nobility of all Christians"). "As you receive this information," he ends, "the Adelantado Bartolomé Colón [his brother] is setting out with three ships well equipped for the purpose, to explore these lands I have newly discovered, and in which I fervently believe the Garden of Eden lies." (No such voyage by his brother is on record, though.)

Of course, Columbus' report was well within traditional medieval lore, in which logic and consistency mattered little. Strange it was that it came from a man who had helped to dispel such lore, and who was writing at the threshold of the sixteenth century, and not in a dark monastery, but from the New World.

Hispaniola Once More

When the Admiral returned to Hispaniola, he found the island in an even worse state than he had left it. The Indians were dying away, silently. The Spaniards had totally fallen out among themselves over the spoils.

Thus the two brothers Bartolomé and Diego, who found

themselves almost without allies among the colonists, were more than happy to welcome Cristóbal back.

Now followed almost two years of "final pacification" of the natives, accompanied by mutinies and fights among the colonists. It hardly seems of much interest who did what to whom. The treatment of the Indians was not an issue among the colonists, although the main rebel, Francisco Roldán, won the help of some caciques with his promise of less tribute and no more slave raids. In the end, the Arawaks made the issue academic by dying out; by then the gold tribute system had already long ended through lack of gold and had been replaced with the repartimiento.

The Genoese triumvirate of the brothers could not hope to stay in power, the less so as the King and Queen saw little of the promised gold, no spices, and slaves so sickly that they died before an honest peso's profit had been made. Presently the Court decided to send out a commissioner with full powers to take over. The man chosen was Francisco de Bobadilla, "a poor and jealous knight," according to Columbus' son. (But Bobadilla stayed only a year, and there is nothing to suggest that jealousy of the Admiral guided his actions.) When he arrived at Santo Domingo after much delay, in August 1500, the first spectacle to catch his eye was that of a number of Spaniards swinging from the gallows. Brother Diego told him there were more to follow, condemned for rebellion against the rule of the brothers.

Bobadilla reprieved the other rebels on the spot, but when Diego refused to release them, he had him locked up aboard his ship. Then followed an investigation. It is not difficult to imagine the bedlam of accusations and counter-accusations, a scene probably more "uncivilized" than anything seen on the island in its pre-Columbian days.

A drawing of Columbus in chains.

At the time, Bartolomé and the Admiral were both in the interior, the former fighting a Spanish rebellion, the latter hunting Indians. The two might have organized a resistance to Bobadilla, but they had few sympathizers among the Spaniards who, moreover, had not been paid in months. They decided to obey the royal patent that Bobadilla sent them and come back to Santo Domingo. There they too were arrested. Eventually the three brothers, together with the dossier collected against them, were sent to Spain for trial, Diego and the Admiral on one ship, Bartolomé on another. Once at sea, the captain of Columbus' ship offered to strike off his prisoner's irons, but the Admiral refused, saying that they had been put there by royal command and that only royal command could take them off. In fact, he nursed his bitterness by keeping those chains with him for the rest of his life and demanding that they be buried with him. How Bartolomé and Diego felt about all this was not recorded.

The passage home was fast, and in late October the brothers landed at Cádiz, where the Admiral made his famed appearance in chains. They were kept under guard in a monastery in Seville.

Six weeks later a royal order arrived for the fetters to be removed, and for the men to present themselves at Court, then in Granada.

The de la Torre Letter

The case that Columbus made for himself at Granada can be reconstructed from the de la Torre letter. This letter, written on the ship home, sums up his defense, or apologia. It was addressed to Juana de la Torre, who had been lady-in-waiting to the Infante Juan (who had died). She had remained at Court, a friend of the Queen, and was obviously considered by the Admiral as a good go-between. Perhaps he felt too wronged to address the Court directly; perhaps that was against etiquette.

"Virtuous Lady! If it is new for me to complain against the world, its habit of treating me evilly is old," the letter begins.

"Of the new heaven and the earth," it says further on, "which our Lord made, as Saint John says in the Book of Revelations, following the words to Isaiah, 'He made me the messenger and he showed me where to go,' all men were unbelieving. But the Lord gave to my Lady the Queen the spirit of understanding and the great courage, and He made her, his beloved Daughter, heiress to it all: I took possession of all these lands in her royal name. . . .

"I would happily give up this Enterprise if I could do so without dishonor to my Queen. But Our Lord's succor and that of the Queen compel me to continue. To give her some relief for the sorrows which death had caused her, I undertook a new voyage to new skies and new lands." (What Columbus is saying is that he went on his third voyage to distract the Queen from her grief over the death of her child, the Infante.)

"I believed that my voyage to [the Gulf of] Paria would give her some comfort because of the pearls, and of the gold of Hispaniola, and I commanded the people to fish for pearls and keep them until I came back for them, I made this agreement with them and I understood them to promise me a bushel and a half of pearls. If I did not write the monarchs of this, the reason was that I wanted to determine the amount of gold first. I should have lost neither the pearls nor my honor if I had followed my own profit and let Hispaniola be bankrupted, or if my titles and privileges had been respected."

The reason for this strange ramble, which follows the most

high-toned religious sentiments, is to be found in a voyage made by that same Hojeda who had laid waste to the Vega Real. Hojeda, with the help of a map drawn by Columbus, had made an independent expedition to the Gulf of Paria. He came back to Spain before Columbus ended his second voyage, with a large number of pearls found around Margarita Island. Columbus was saying that those were really his pearls.

Hojeda had been accompanied on that trip by a Florentine from Seville, Amerigo Vespucci. Vespucci's marvelous descriptions of this and other voyages gave him such fame that his name, Amerigo, ended up on the maps of the new continent as "America." This whim of fate (and of a German mapmaker) is often commented upon. But in our age, when the reporter more and more overshadows the events he is reporting, it seems more and more appropriate to me. And I think we must call ourselves lucky that this hemisphere was not named Columbia.

(It may be noted here how many of these "first voyages" were led by men from the banking towns of Italy. Columbus was from Genoa, Vespucci and Verrazano from Florence, John Cabot from Venice. The great discoveries have been called "the last great adventure of the Mediterraneans.")

Columbus' defense continues by relating how the various colonists rejected his leadership—"adventurers all, not one man with wife and children," he adds somewhat unfairly.

He calls Bobadilla a wicked man, whose first act was "to take the gold, without measuring or weighing it and in my absence. He said he was going to pay the people from it and as I hear he took the first part for himself. . . . I had put aside, for the monarchs' pleasure, many samples of gold, nuggets as large as a goose or a hen's eggs, to show them the trade can be profitable. . . . Bobadilla's first malicious trick was to hold these samples back, so that the monarchs should give little importance to the gold collecting, until he had feathered his own nest, which he is doing fast. The gold, stored for melting down, has become less in the fire. . . .

"In Spain, they judge me as if I had been governor of Sicily or of a province or city under an established government, and where the laws can be observed without fear of chaos. This is most unjust. I should be judged as a captain sent from Spain to the Indies to conquer a numerous and warlike people. . . ."

Thus were described those vanishing Arawaks, about whom the Admiral had once said, "They still remain incurably timid. True, when they have been reassured and lost their fear, they are so naive and so free with their possessions that no one who has not witnessed them would believe it. When you ask for something they have, they never say no. . . ."

"The gate is open for gold and pearls," the Admiral then wrote, "and we can expect large quantities of precious stones, spices, and other things. I pray that no new calamity will befall me, and that I can now undertake the voyage to open up our trade with Arabia Felix as far as Mecca. And then I will go to Calicut.

"On Christmas Day, the Lord miraculously comforted me, saying, 'Take courage, be not afraid, I will provide for everything, the seven years of the gold concessions have not run out.'" This divine statement about gold concessions is not clear to me, but the Admiral goes on to say that, on that same day, he heard there were three hundred and fifty miles of land on Hispaniola containing (gold) mines from end to end: "nay, all that is one single mine. . . ."

And with a rather direct hint to the King and Queen, he ends, "The Lord God still holds power and wisdom as in the days of old, and punishes all wrongs, and ingratitude foremost."

8

THE LAST MOVE

As the voyage of Hojeda and Vespucci showed, the Enterprise of the Indies was now being carried by its own momentum. Its originator, Columbus, and his brothers were received at Court, and Columbus succeeded in having his titles of admiral and viceroy confirmed once more. But it was understood that these were now honorific and did not carry any further authority. The "action" shifted to others. In fact, when Nicolás de Ovando was sent out as successor to Bobadilla, Columbus was not consulted and no one suggested he go along. Ovando sailed in the largest contingent yet, thirty-one ships with 2,500 hundred men.

It was to become Ovando's role to erase the final traces of Indian society. He was received by the female cacique Anacoana, who had brought together all other remaining chiefs, eighty-four of them, to welcome him. Setting an example later followed by Cortes and Pizarro, the Spaniards fell upon the unsuspecting crowd, burned down Anacoana's house with all who were inside, killed the others, and hanged Anacoana.

Thus Hispaniola fell silent, and would a few years later provide a thoroughly safe base from which to mete out the same treatment to the Indian population of Cuba.

Meanwhile Columbus spent two years arguing and demanding that he be given one more chance to reach Cathay. He was met with a somewhat embarrassed no. It was agreed that Bobadilla had been too harsh with him, but no one saw much point in giving him new ships. For five years now, since 1495, Spanish ships had been making explorations westward without a by-your-leave from the Admiral. Nothing he had done since had increased confidence in him.

But Vasco da Gama's successful voyage was followed by another one, in the year 1500, in which Cabral took a fleet of Portuguese ships east, made a landfall in what is now Brazil, and then reached India. After him, da Gama made another voyage. Henry the Navigator's plan had succeeded: the sea route to the East Indies was established, and the monopoly of the Italian merchant towns ended. Portugal was the nation that had done it and was to inherit the key to this economic power.

The Court of Spain finally agreed to let Columbus try once more to do what he insisted he could and would do. In fact, he announced he would meet da Gama in the East Indian seas, and accordingly he took a royal letter with him, not addressed this time to the Grand Khan, but to Vasco da Gama: "We inform him [da Gama] of your [Columbus'] voyage to the West, as we have been informed of his voyage to the East. If you should meet at sea, you should treat each other in a friendly way, as befits captains and subjects of kings bound together by such kinship, love, and affection." Then as later, Spain and Portugal were determined to stick to the line of Tordesillas and keep the peace overseas. But if the East Indies could be reached by going west, beyond that line, Spain would not be trespassing according to the treaty.

To avoid new incidents and arguments, a royal notary was to go with Columbus to draw up a list of all gold, silver, pearls, and so forth, and Columbus was expressly forbidden, one, to call at Hispaniola and, two, to entertain any recriminations or charges on his return. He was to treat his crew as "royal servants" and was not to bring back any slaves.

He accepted all these conditions, and sailed with four ships in May 1502. Aboard were a considerable complement of experienced pilots and navigators, as well as his brother Bartolomé (who came unwillingly) and his son Hernando. One captain was Pedro de Terrenos, the only man known to have sailed on all four voyages (he had begun his career as Columbus' servant); another was Bartolomeo Fieschi, a prominent Genoese. Fieschi's command suggests that it was not just Columbus' Genoese origin that had created so much ill will against him (as he and his family liked to claim).

This fourth voyage was in a sense a silent admission by the Admiral that he had—contrary to all his reports—not yet found the Golden East. He had been east (Hispaniola), northwest (Cuba), and south (Trinidad). Both off Cuba and off Margarita Island, he had turned around and gone back, as if determined to leave the issue open rather than run the risk of being proven wrong.

And this last voyage, which led him to the coast of Central America, would once more be broken off inconclusively. And the Admiral once more topped it with a report about fabulous riches within reach, and about landfalls "on the borders of Cathay."

A String of Disasters

A very swift crossing took the ships from the Canaries to Martinique, where they renewed their water supply. The Admiral was already complaining in the log about his crew and his ships and—as probably could be expected, given his frame of mind—called next at Santo Domingo, although this had been forbidden. The reasons he gave were that he wanted to exchange one of his ships for another, and that he wanted to find shelter against a storm brewing. Ovando refused him permission to land, which served him for one of his now frequent bouts of self-pity, or, as it might now be called, persecution anxiety. "What man has not been born," he later wrote to the King and Queen, "including Job himself, who would not have died of despair when in such a storm he should be forbidden to land, for his own safety and that of his little son, and brother, and shipmates, land that, by God's will, I had sweated blood for, to acquire for Spain?"

This passage set the tone for an ever more intense rage. Columbus, now in his early fifties, was from then on not really a rational commander, as his writings of the time show. Perhaps, as G.R. Crone suggests, his brother Bartolomé virtually took over. However that may be, the fourth voyage became a string of calamities—with most of the victims, as always, the native population.

Not many of the incidents in this voyage are of more than historical-geographical interest. After riding out the storm (in which his enemy Bobadilla, on his way to Spain, perished), the ships called on Cuba and then set course for the Central American coast, which was sighted in September 1502 at the latitude of sixteen degrees north. The only account of this crossing is in Columbus' *Lettera rarissema,* a long and indeed hysterical letter he wrote the following year (from Jamaica) to the King and Queen.

The letter throws a harsh light on Columbus' state of mind, but it is of little use in tracing the voyage, for all events and distances are fantastically distorted and exaggerated. It is filled with visions, and God Himself repeatedly addresses the Admiral, compares him to Moses and David, and tells him to go on believing in himself (and in his monarchs). Columbus reports, once again, gold mines beyond belief, in Veragua (now Panama) this time, and announces that no one but he will be able to find his way back to that magic place. He keeps swearing to the truth of this "gold without limit" and of the Ganges River ten days' sailing away.

Trivial and even petty details are followed by passages such as, "Gold is the most excellent, gold is treasure, and who has it can do whatever he likes in this world. With it, he can bring

The New World ("Mondo Novo") as Columbus saw it after four voyages. This sketch is by Venetian geographer Allesandro Zorzi, who probably copied it in the 1520s from a map by Bartolomé Columbus. Note how "Mondo Novo" is part of Asia.

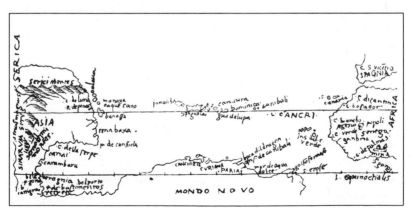

souls to Paradise. . . . Solomon was brought 666 talents of gold [one "talent" was about one thousand ounces of gold] from one expedition, apart from what he received from merchants and sailors and from the Arabs. With this he made two hundred spears and three hundred shields, and he covered his throne with solid gold and precious stones. . . . Josephus [historian from the first century A.D.] believes this gold came from Aureau. If that is true, the gold fields of Aureau are in my opinion the same as those of Veragua which, as I said, are twenty days' journey to the west. . . . Solomon bought all this gold, precious stones, and silver, but your Majesties may order them to be collected freely at your pleasure."

These outbursts, inspired as they were by nothing more than a coast of jungle, usually hidden in a sheaf of rain, are indeed baffling. Quoting them, I am assuredly not trying to make fun of Columbus, if only because there was too much death and cruelty in his wake to find anything funny in such ravings.

Thus, I am haunted by a petty incident, though it fades into nothingness when compared to the thousands of men, women, and children killed. It happened somewhere off Costa Rica, and Columbus himself thought fit to describe it in his letter to the monarchs. "There are many animals here, large and small," he writes, "and different from ours. I took aboard two pigs [the American peccary] which scared the Irish wolfhound [who was aboard for the hunting of Indians]. A crossbowman wounded an animal like an ape, but large and with a human face [probably a spider monkey]. He had pierced him with an arrow from breast to tail, but still had to cut off his front and hind foot because he was so fierce. When one of the pigs saw this monkey, it bristled and fled. When I noticed this, I ordered the *begare,* as the natives call this ape, to be thrown to the pig. Although he was dying, with the arrow still all through his body, he coiled his tail around the pig's head as soon as he got near him, held him very tight and with his remaining forefoot hit him hard on the head, as if he were his enemy."

It may be objected that this was a cruel age; we may be reminded of bear baiting or bull fights. Throwing a dying monkey and a wild pig together seems something else again, though. I find it sad to think about this commander of men who took pleasure in such a thing, and who wrote about it in his report to his king.

The tacking east of the ships along that coast, to Cape Gracias a Dios (on the border of what are now Honduras and Nicaragua) makes a monotonous tale. From there, with the land falling away sharply to the south, better progress was made. At Belén (seventy miles west of where the Panama Canal now begins) a base was set up from which to explore those alleged gold fields of Veragua.

Here the Navidad tragedy was once more played out. Raids inland for gold and food soon changed the Indians from friendly to hostile. ("One Spaniard eats as much in a day as a family of Indians in a month," de las Casas would later write.) The Admiral had planned to go on to Hispaniola and leave Bartolomé behind in command of a fort. Once more the local cacique and fifty other hostages were captured, and taken away on the ships.

There were skirmishes, and Columbus' position was further complicated by terrible weather. One night some of his captives succeeded in escaping from his ship and swimming ashore, while the remaining hostages, to frustrate the Spaniards in their purpose, committed suicide by hanging themselves from the beams in the low hold. "Their deaths were no great harm to the ships," Columbus' son calmly noted; while Morison, four and a half centuries later, equally calmly writes (as if he were talking of a sports event), "Those who did not escape managed to hang themselves from the deck beams while confined in the hold."

The plan for a fort was finally abandoned and three of the ships set sail for Santo Domingo. One was lost. It was now early summer of 1503, and with much argument between the pilots, and much swearing by the crew, which was pumping day and night to keep the leaky vessels afloat, a landfall was made on Jamaica, at Saint Ann's Bay on the north coast, where the ships were beached. And there the ship's company remained stuck for a year.

That year in Jamaica added nothing to the knowledge of geography. As a tale of fights and intrigues, it is a dreary repetition of the past. As always, Columbus' companions turned against him and against each other. Various cliques formed, and the rumor was spread that he had been exiled and did not really want to leave. An emissary was sent to Hispaniola to ask for help. Ovando, undisputed ruler there, was in no hurry to fetch Columbus. When months later he finally sent a vessel, its captain gave the marooned company some victuals but refused to take anyone aboard. Not until their emissary managed to charter a caravel in Santo Domingo at his own expense were the men taken from Jamaica to Hispaniola.

Indeed, it seems amazing that in all those months they did not succeed in repairing one of their ships, or building a boat, for the crossing to Hispaniola. Nor did they even try to feed themselves with, for instance, fish. As always, it was the unhappy natives who had to feed the invaders of their land.

Now, for the reader of these chronicles, numbness sets in. You read of attempts by mutinous officers to get away on their own in Indian canoes. The brothers Diego and Franco Porras, for instance, tried that. They turned around when the seas got too rough for their taste, and to lighten the boat, they simply threw their Indian rowers overboard. Those who clung to the gunwales had their hands chopped off and vanished in the waves. You feel numb, you feel a pain of nonbelieving. It would be wrong to say the Spaniards were bestial. Beasts do not know of cruelty; they are innocent creatures following their nature-given instincts.

The company arrived back in Santo Domingo in August 1504. Most chose to stay there for the time being. The Admiral, his son, brother, and some others, took passage for home. In November they were back in Spain, landing downstream from Seville. Columbus' voyages were over.

Before he left behind him the last of those Indians who had danced and offered thanks to heaven when they first laid eyes on white men, he wrote to the King and Queen, "Alone in my miseries, infirm, daily expecting death, and surrounded by a million hostile savages full of cruelty. . . . Weep for me who has charity, truth, and justice!"

9

CLOSING THE LEDGER

The Admiral had written to his monarchs, while still in Jamaica, that the one thing he now desired was to make a pilgrimage to Rome and other holy places. That was probably only one more broadside fired for effect, for back in Spain his only quest till his dying day was to get satisfaction for his various claims and grievances. It must be said that he was in poor health and had less than two years to live: dying, in the words of his son, "from gout and other ills, and from grief at seeing himself so fallen from his high estate," in Valladolid in May 1506.

But the picture of the Admiral ending his life poor and forgotten is false. Queen Isabella had died in the autumn of 1505. King Ferdinand, supposedly Columbus' enemy, treated him better than one might have expected from that very matter–of–fact ruler.

Columbus had stated that his honor was his first considera-tion, and honor was satisfied. His hereditary title of Admiral of the Ocean was once more confirmed, and so was, more surprisingly, his viceroyalty. That title was transferred to his son Diego, who moreover received the King's permission to marry a lady from the highest aristocracy. (Under the original Capitulations, the viceroyalty was not to be inherited.)

The matter of money was something else. Columbus now not only claimed his one-tenth of all gold found in the Indies, but even dug up legal precedent for a share of one-third of all trade with that region. The King suggested that the matter be settled by arbitration, which the Admiral refused.

It seems futile to me to spend much thought on who had "the right" to those treasures stolen from a far country and collected at a most terrible price in innocent blood. The original Capitulations indeed granted Columbus his tenth, but they had been drawn up with the idea of a trading station off the coast of Japan, not a new world. What King Ferdinand finally granted him was one-tenth of the royal fifth, or two percent, and that was enough to make him a very rich man.

10

COLUMBUS DAY

It lies within our comfortable liberal tradition that we don't like events to be depicted in stark colors. We like shadings. We particularly don't like things or people to be written up as all bad. Everything has its nuances, we claim. Only fanatics and extremists fail to see that.

Mankind and womankind, sitting (still rather well-fed) in their (still rather well-heated) rooms, feel a considerable tenderness toward themselves.

Upperdog, mostly white, mankind, that is. And throughout its bloody history, mankind has labelled as fanatics, agitators, and troublemakers all those who have felt less tender and rosy about the world.

Well, fanatical and extreme as it may be, I find it very hard to think of any shadings or nuances in a character portrait of Christopher Columbus.

Grant him the originality and fierce ambition needed to set that western course. But what else is there to say? Here was a man greedy in large ways, and in small ways—to the point where he took for himself the reward for first sighting land from the Pinta lookout. Cruel in petty things, as when he set a dying monkey with two paws cut off to fight a wild pig; cruel on a continental scale, as when he set in motion what de las Casas called "the beginning of the bloody trail of conquest across the Americas."

We may try to redeem him by stating that he was a man of his time. That is certainly true. And it is to the greater glory of those men who were not "of their time": de las Casas, who in vain fought for half a century to save the Indians; Antonio de Montesinos, a Dominican friar who preached in Santo Domingo in 1511, "I am a voice crying in the wilderness." (He was recalled shortly thereafter.) It would be the lives of those very few men who would, it such were possible, save the honor of that Holy Faith in whose name a continental massacre was committed.

There were a few worldly men around, too, who were not "of their time." Pedro Margarit, who sickened at the treatment of the Arawaks, who left Hispaniola and spoke against Columbus at Court. In another theater, a man such as the Portuguese Alfonso de Albuquerque, who treated his subjects in Portuguese India as if they were people.

But men like these were pathetically few in number, and *still are*. The Spaniards cut off the hands of the Arawaks who didn't come in with enough gold. More than four hundred years later, Brazilian entrepreneurs cut off the ears of the Indians who didn't come in with enough wild rubber. The Spaniards threw the Indian children in the sea, shouting, "Boil in hell, children of the devil." The United States General Westmoreland announced, "An Oriental does not prize his life like we do." He used new and improved napalm, while the Spaniards in Hispaniola used green wood for burning the Indian caciques in order to make them suffer and scream longer—as an example for the others, of course.

In what is now the United States, the Indians were destroyed no less effectively than in Hispaniola. In Brazil, it is going on even now. Perhaps the only exceptions were the Indians of the Canadian wilderness; and only here was there no economic premium on their extermination.

Perhaps we will come to say that Columbus was not only a man of his time, but that he was a man of his race.

The word "race" may no longer be accepted in science because it cannot properly be defined. That does not prevent us all from knowing quite well what is meant by "the white race"; but let us say then that Columbus was a typical man of the (white) West. And the West has ravaged the world for five hundred years, under the flag of a master-slave theory which in our finest hour of hypocrisy was called "the white man's burden." Perhaps the Master-Race Nazis were different from the rest of us, mostly in the sense that they extended that theory to their fellow whites. (In doing so, they did the subject races of this world a favor. The great white-race civil war which we call World War II weakened Europe and broke its grip on Asia and Africa.) I am not ignoring the cruelties of other races. They were usually less hypocritical, though; they were not, in Marx's phrase, "civilization mongers" as they laid waste to other lands. But they too fill the pages of history with man's inhumanity to man.

What sets the West apart is its persistence, its capacity to *stop at nothing*. No other race or religion or nonreligion ever quite matched the Christian West in that respect. Of course those others did not as a rule have the technology and the means to go on and on. The West did, and does—that same persistence has given it its power for good and for bad. We may end then by saying that Columbus was but one frightening example of the corruption of unchecked power, such as precisely the West used to wield.

And there was nothing to check the Spaniards, whose steel, horses, and gunpowder made them invulnerable. Any check on their power would have had to come from inside themselves. Inside themselves was lust for gain and the Christian faith. The two did not appear to be in conflict.

Undoubtedly, the Spaniards were Christians. But that manifested itself in surprising ways. De las Casas reports how they made low, wide gallows on which they strung up the Arawaks, their feet almost touching the ground. Then they put burning green wood at their feet. These executions took place in lots of thirteen. Thirteen Arawaks were hanged each time. Why? This was "in memory of Our Redeemer and His twelve Apostles."

De las Casas continues to say that chiefs and nobles were usually not hanged like that, but burned to death on grids of rods. Once, he writes, a captain complained that he couldn't sleep because of the cries and he ordered the victims strangled. But the constable ("and I know his name and the names of his family in Seville") instead put sticks over their tongues so that they could not make a sound, and "roasted them slowly, as he liked." Men, women, and children on Columbus' Hispaniola were hacked to pieces, and those pieces were sold from stalls to the Spaniards for feeding their dogs. It was considered good military policy to give these dogs a taste for Indians.

De Bry, an etcher from the Dutch Lowlands, has illustrated the conquest. Those faces, under the pointed helmets, with the little triangular beards, look on coldly as the Indians are strangled, burned, and cut down. They are the stuff of nightmares.

The curse of the conquest still lies over most of Latin America. Here the encomiendas continue in a more subtle form, and the very few still own the very many.

South of the United States border, October 12 is now commemorated as "the day of the race." The race, that is, as it now exists, of mixed Spanish and Indian and African stock.

You cannot find fault with that. That race, *la raza,* is a reality. These children of conquerors and slaves are the only achievement of the conquest, the only wealth it produced. For all the gold and silver stolen and shipped to Spain did not make the Spanish people richer. It gave their kings an edge in the balance of power for a time, a chance to hire more mercenary soldiers for their wars. They ended up losing those wars, anyway, and all that was left was a deadly inflation, a starving population, the rich richer, the poor poorer, and a ruined peasant class.

Perhaps in the children of *la raza* lies the hope for a final reconciliation of this war that Europe and its white outposts have waged on America and Africa.

But up north we call October 12 "Columbus Day." Are we committed then to continue in that bloody track? Shouldn't we try to have our thoughts, on the anniversary of the day it all began, run in a new direction? Shouldn't we change that name?

Our false heroes have long burdened our history and our character.

Shouldn't we wind up that Enterprise of Columbus and start thinking of a truly New World?

A BIBLIOGRAPHY

It may exist, but I have not found one elementary school or high-school book that does not treat Columbus as the great hero he was not. Perhaps it is only natural that authors outside the United States write more calmly about him. Bjoern Landstrom's book, *Columbus,* gives many interesting technical details of his ships and crews (New York: Macmillan, 1967). *The Four Voyages of Christopher Columbus,* edited by John Michael Cohen (Baltimore: Penguin Books, 1969), is a fine paperback giving a continuous story, using the writings and journals of Columbus' contemporaries and of his son. More scholarly (but exciting, not dry) is G. R. Crone's *The Discovery of America,* to which this book of mine owes a great debt (London: Hamish Hamilton, 1969).

Sadly, none of these books are in print at the time I am writing this bibliography (in late 1990), but good public and school libraries will have some or all.

If John Michael Cohen's paperback makes you feel ready to go to the source, much of it has been translated in English: the journals, Columbus' life story written by his son Hernando, and the writings of Bartolomé de las Casas. Hernando Colón's *Life of Christopher Columbus* was published by Greenwood Press (Westport, CT), and is still in print. There are many versions of the journals; watch out, because some of the published material is spurious, written later by others. In print in English are: *The Diario of the First Voyage,* published by the University of Oklahoma Press, and *Four Voyages,* published by the Peter Smith Publishing House (Magnolia, MA).

I already mentioned many times in my story the books of de las Casas, the friar, later bishop of Chiapas, who was the first to alert the world to what was happening in the West Indies. His *Account of the First Voyages . . . the Unparalleled Cruelties. . .* and his *Destrucción de las Indias* (*Devastation of the Indies*) have been in print in many languages since the seventeenth century—which makes it somewhat awkward to say, "We didn't know." (Tragically, de las Casas could think of no other way to save the Indians than by suggesting that slaves from Africa, who were supposedly physically stronger, should be imported. The Indians died anyway; as for the stronger Africans, it was estimated in the year 1800 that three million black slaves in the United States were the sole surviving descendants of twenty million slaves captured and imported into that same area. Bartolomé de las Casas' *Devastation of the Indies* was published in a new translation by Seabury Press (New York, 1974); it is not in print. A selection of his writings was published by Knopf (New York, 1971).

Then there is Samuel Eliot Morison, who long held a kind of American monopoly on Columbus. Admiral Morison had followed the voyages in a yacht and knew much about currents, storms, landfalls and all, but he showed no perception of the age and of the role of Columbus in it. His books make Columbus and his men sound like hearty, gallant, Chamber of

Commerce trade boosters, carrying good sense and jolly Christianity to a new continent. In one of my favorite passages, Morison rhapsodizes about the delights of the first cup of coffee on an early morning at sea, adding as a lame afterthought that the Spaniards didn't know coffee yet.

If you are ready to read about Columbus in a wider context, of the background of Spain and the increasingly tragic story of the native Americans, and, later, of the slaves brought to America, there are a number of titles in which the traditional image of Columbus as the blue-eyed hero has been abandoned for a more historical one.

Eduardo Galeano's three-volume *Memory of Fire* (New York: Pantheon, 1988) takes the story of Latin America from its first known inhabitants to the present time. The same author's *Open Veins of Latin America* (New York: Monthly Review Press, 1973) has become a classic account of the continent's historic exploitation.

A. Crosby's *The Columbian Exchange* (Westport, CT: Greenwood Press, 1972) is an original investigation of who gave what to whom, what Europeans gave and took, what the Indians gave, and suffered. This is also the subject of *Indian Givers,* by Jack Weatherford (New York: Crown, 1988).

Robert Berkhofer, in his *The White Man's Indian, History of an Idea from Columbus to the Present* (New York: Knopf, 1978), deals with the comfortable stereotypes in which the white man could wrap his misdeeds. The same point of view dominates *Who's the Savage?* by D. R. Wrone and R. S. Nelson (New York: Fawcett, 1973). It is also dealt with in the scholarly *Origins of the American Indians: European Concepts, 1492-1729,* by Lee Huddleston (San Antonio: University of Texas Press, 1967).

Lastly, an overall view on bias and historical myths, written especially for teachers, is *Thinking and Rethinking U.S. History,* edited by Gerald Horne and available from the Council on Interracial Books for Children, 1841 Broadway, New York, NY 10023.

COLUMBUS IN THE CLASSROOM

by Bill Bigelow

Most of my students have trouble with the idea that a book—especially a *textbook*—can lie. When I tell them that I want them to argue with, not just read, the printed word they're not sure what I mean. That's why I start my U.S. history class by stealing a student's purse.

As the year opens, my students may not know when the Civil War was fought, what James Madison or Frederick Douglass did, or where the Underground Railroad went, but they do know that a brave fellow named Christopher Columbus discovered America. Okay, the Vikings may have actually *discovered* America, but students know it was Columbus who mapped it and *did* something with the place. Indeed, this bit of historical lore may be the only knowledge class members share in common.

What students don't know is that year after year their textbooks have, by omission or otherwise, been lying to them on a grand scale. Some students learned that Columbus sailed on three ships and that his sailors worried whether they would ever see land again. Others know from readings and teachers that when the Admiral landed he was greeted by naked, reddish skinned people whom he called Indians. And still others may know Columbus gave these people little trinkets and returned to Spain with a few of the Indians to show King Ferdinand and Queen Isabella.

All this is true. What is also true is that Columbus took hundreds of Indians slaves and sent them back to Spain, where most of them were sold and subsequently died. What is also true is that in his quest for gold Columbus had the hands cut off any Indian who did not return with his or her three month quota. And what is also true is that on one island alone, Hispaniola, an entire race of people was wiped off the face of the earth in a mere forty years of Spanish administration.

So I begin by stealing a student's purse. I announce to the class that the purse is mine, Obviously, because look who has it. Most students are fair-minded. They saw me take the purse off the desk, so they protest: "That's not yours, it's Nikki's. You took it, we saw you." I brush these objections aside and reiterate that it is mine, and to prove it I'll show them all the things I have inside.

I unzip the bag and remove a brush or a comb, maybe a pair of dark glasses. A tube, or whatever it's called, of lipstick works best: "This is my lipstick," I say. "There, that proves it *is* my purse." They don't buy it and, in fact, are mildly outraged that I would pry into someone's possessions with such utter disregard for her privacy. (I've alerted the student to the demonstration before class, but no one else knows that.)

It's time to move on: "Okay, if it's Nikki's purse, how do you know? Why are you all so positive it's not my purse?" Different answers: We saw you take it; that's her lipstick, we know you don't wear lipstick; there is stuff in there with her name on it. To get the point across, I even offer to help in their effort to prove Nikki's possession: "If we had a test on the contents of the purse, who would do better, Nikki or me?" "Whose labor earned the money that bought the things in the purse, mine or Nikki's?" Obvious questions, obvious answers.

I make one last try to keep Nikki's purse: "What if I said I *discovered* this purse, then would it be mine?" A little laughter is my reward, but I don't get any takers; they still think the purse is rightfully Nikki's.

"So," I ask, "why do we say that Columbus discovered America?" Now they begin to see what I've been leading up to. I ask a series of rhetorical questions which implicitly make the link between Nikki's purse and the Indians' land: Were there people on the land before Columbus arrived? Who had been on the land longer, Columbus or the Indians? Who knew the land better? Who had put their labor into making the land produce? The students see where I'm going—it would be hard not to. "And yet," I continue, "what is the first thing that Columbus did when he arrived in the New World?" Right: he took possession of it. After all, he had discovered the place.

We talk about phrases other than "discovery" that textbooks could use to describe what Columbus did. Students start with the phrases they used to describe what I did to Nikki's purse: he stole it; he took it; he ripped it off. And others: he invaded it; he conquered it.

I want students to see that the word "discovery" is loaded. The word carries with it a perspective, a bias; it takes sides. "Discovery" is the phrase of the supposed discoverers. It's the conquerors, the invaders, masking their theft. And when the word gets repeated in textbooks those textbooks become, in the phrase of one historian, "the propaganda of the winners."

To prepare students to examine critically the textbooks of their past, we begin with some alternative, and rather unsentimental, explorations of Columbus' "enterprise," as he called it. The Admiral-to-be was not sailing for mere adventure and to prove the world was round, as my fourth grade teacher had informed her class, but to secure the tremendous profits that were to be made by reaching the Indies. From the beginning, Columbus' quest was wealth, both for Spain and for himself personally. He demanded a 10 percent cut of everything shipped to Spain via the western route—and not just for himself but for all his heirs in perpetuity. And he insisted he be pronounced governor of any new lands he found, a title that carried with it dictatorial powers.

Mostly I want the class to think about the human beings Columbus was to "discover"—and then destroy. I read from a letter Columbus wrote, dated March 14, 1493, following his return from the first voyage. He reports being enormously impressed by the indigenous people:

> As soon . . . as they see that they are safe and have laid aside all fear, they are very simple and honest and exceedingly liberal with all they have; none of them refusing anything he may possess when he is asked for it, but, on the contrary, inviting us to ask them. They exhibit great love toward all others in preference to themselves. They also give objects of great value for trifles, and content themselves with very little or nothing in return. . . . I did not find, as some of us had expected, any cannibals among them, but, on the contrary, men of great deference and kindness.[1]

But, on an ominous note, Columbus writes in his log, ". . . should your Majesties command it, all the inhabitants could be taken away to Castile [Spain], or made slaves on the island. With fifty men we could subjugate them all and make them do whatever we want."[2]

I ask students if they remember from elementary school days what it was Columbus brought back with him from his travels in the New World. Together students recall that he brought back parrots, plants, some gold, and a few of the people Columbus had taken to calling "Indians." This was Columbus' first expedition and it is also where most school textbook accounts of Columbus end—conveniently. Because the enterprise of Columbus was not to bring back exotic knickknacks, but riches, preferably gold. What about his second voyage?

I read to them a passage from this fine book, Hans Koning's *Columbus: His Enterprise:*

> We are now in February 1495. Time was short for sending back a good "dividend" on the supply ships getting ready for the return to Spain. Columbus therefore turned to a massive slave raid as a means for filling up these ships. The brothers [Columbus and his brothers, Bartolomé and Diego] rounded up fifteen hundred Arawaks—men, women, and children— and imprisoned them in pens in Isabela, guarded by men and dogs. The ships had room for no more than five hundred, and thus only the best specimens were loaded aboard. The Admiral then told the Spaniards they could help themselves from the remainder to as many slaves as they wanted. Those whom no one chose were simply kicked out of their pens. Such had been the terror of these prisoners that (in the description by Michele de Cuneo, one of the colonists) "they rushed in all directions like lunatics, women dropping and abandoning infants in the rush, running for miles without stopping, fleeing across moun- tains and rivers."
>
> Of the five hundred slaves, three hundred arrived alive in Spain, where they were put up for sale in Seville by Don Juan de Fonseca, the archdeacon of the town. "As naked as the day they

were born," the report of this excellent churchman says, *"but with no more embarrassment than animals. . ."*

The slave trade immediately turned out to be "unprofitable, for the slaves mostly died." Columbus decided to concentrate on gold, although he writes, "Let us *in the name of the Holy Trinity* go on sending all the slaves that can be sold.[3]

Certainly Columbus' fame should not be limited to the discovery of America: he also deserves credit for initiating the trans–Atlantic slave trade, albeit in the opposite direction than we're used to thinking of it.

Students and I role-play a scene from Columbus' second voyage. Slavery is not producing the profits Columbus is seeking. He still believes there is gold in them thar hills and the Indians are selfishly holding out on him. Students play Columbus; I play the Indians: "Chris, we don't have any gold, honest. Can we go back to living our lives now and you can go back to wherever you came from?" I call on several students to respond to the Indians' plea. Columbus thinks the Indians are lying. How can he get his gold? Student responses range from sympathetic to ruthless: Okay, we'll go home; *please* bring us your gold; we'll lock you up in prison if you don't bring us your gold; we'll torture you if you don't fork it over, etc. After I've pleaded for awhile and the students-as-Columbus have threatened, I real aloud another passage from Koning's book describing the system Columbus arrived at for extracting gold from the Indians:

Every man and woman, every boy or girl of fourteen or older, in the province of Cibao (of the imaginary gold fields) had to collect gold for the Spaniards. As their measure, the Spaniards used . . . hawks' bells. . . . Every three months, every Indian had to bring to one of the forts a hawks' bell filled with gold dust. The chiefs had to bring in about ten times that amount. In the other provinces of Hispaniola, twenty-five pounds of spun cotton took the place of gold.

Copper tokens were manufactured, and when an Indian had brought his or her tribute to an armed post, he or she received such a token, stamped with the month, to be hung around the neck. With that they were safe for another three months while collecting more gold.

Whoever was caught without a token was killed by having his or her hands cut off. There are old Spanish prints . . . that show this being done: the Indians stumble away, staring *with surprise* at their arm stumps pulsing out blood.

There were no gold fields, and thus, once the Indians had handed in whatever they still had in gold ornaments, their only hope was to work all day in the streams, washing out gold dust from the pebbles. It was an impossible task, but those Indians who tried to flee into the mountains were systematically hunted down with dogs and killed, to set an example for the others to keep trying. . . .

Thus it was at this time that the mass suicides began: the Arawaks killed themselves with cassava poison.

During those two years of the administration of the brothers Columbus, an estimated one half of the entire population of Hispaniola was killed or killed themselves. The estimates run from 125,000 to one-half million.[4]

It's important that students not be shielded from the horror of what "discovery" meant to its victims. The fuller they understand the consequences of Columbus' invasion of America, the better they'll be equipped to critically reexamine the innocent stories their textbooks have offered through the years. The goal is not to titillate or stun, but to force the question: Why wasn't I told this before?

Students' assignment is to find a textbook, preferably one

they used in elementary school (but any textbook will suffice) and write a critique of the book's treatment of Columbus and the Indians. I distribute the following handout to students and review the questions aloud. I don't want them to merely answer the questions one by one, but to consider them as guidelines in completing their critiques:

—How factually accurate was the account?

—What was omitted—left out—that in your judgment would be important for a full understanding of Columbus? (For example, his treatment of the Indians; slave trading; his method of getting gold; the overall effect on the Indians.)

—What motives does the book give to Columbus? Compare those with his real motives.

—Who does the book get you to root for, and how do they accomplish that? (For example, is the book horrified at the treatment of Indians or thrilled that Columbus makes it to the New World?)

—What function do pictures play in the book? What do they communicate about Columbus and his "enterprise"?

—In your opinion, *why* does the book portray the Columbus/Indian encounter the way it does?

—Can you think of any groups in our society that might have an interest in people having an inaccurate view of history?

I tell students that this last question is tough but crucial. Is the continual distortion of Columbus simply an accident, repeated innocently over and over, or are there groups in our society that could benefit from everyone's having a false or limited understanding of the past? Whether or not students are able to answer the question effectively, it is still important that they struggle with it before our group discussion of their critiques.

The subtext of the assignment is to teach students that text material, indeed all written material, is to be read skeptically. I want students to explore the politics of print, that perspectives on history and social reality underlie the written word and that to read is not only to comprehend what is written, but also to question *why* it is written. My intention is not to encourage an "I-don't-believe-anything" cynicism,[5] but rather to equip students to bring the writer's assumptions and values to the surface so that they can decide what is useful and what is not in any particular work.

For practice, we look at some excerpts from a textbook that belonged to my brother in the fourth grade in California, *The Story of American Freedom* (Macmillan, 1964). Students and I real aloud and analyze several paragraphs. The arrival of Columbus and crew is especially revealing—and obnoxious. As is true in every book on the "discovery" I've ever encountered, the reader watches events from the Spaniards' point of view. We are told how Columbus and his men "fell upon their knees and gave thanks to God," a passage included in virtually all elementary school accounts of Columbus. "He then took possession of it [the island] in the name of King Ferdinand and Queen Isabella of Spain."[6] No question is raised of what right Columbus had to assume control over a land which was obviously already occupied by people. The account is so adoring, so respectful of the Admiral, that students can't help but sense the book is offering approval for what is, quite simply, an act of naked imperialism.

The book keeps us close to God and church throughout its narrative. Upon returning from the New World, Columbus shows off his parrots and Indians (again no question of the propriety of the unequal relationship between "natives" and colonizers), and immediately following the show, "the king and queen lead the way to a near-by church. There a song of praise and thanksgiving is sung."[7] Intended or not, the function of linking church and Columbus is to remove him and his actions still further from question and critique. My job, on the other hand, is to encourage students to pry beneath every phrase and illustration; to begin to train readers who can both understand the word and challenge it.

I give students a week before I ask them to bring in their written critiques. In small groups, they share their papers with one another. I ask them to take notes toward what my co-teacher Linda Christensen and I call the "collective text": What themes seem to recur in the papers and what important differences emerge?

Here are some excerpts from papers written this year by students in the Literature and U.S. History course that Linda and I co-teach.

Maryanne wrote:

> "In 1492 Columbus sailed the ocean blue." He ran into a land mass claiming it in the name of Spain. The next day Columbus went ashore. "Indians," almost naked, greeted Columbus who found them a simple folk who "invite you to share anything they possess." Columbus observed that "fifty Spaniards could subjugate this entire people." Then we are told, "By 1548 the Indians were almost all wiped out."—from a passage in *The Impact of Our Past.*
>
> That story is about as complete as swiss cheese. Columbus and the Spaniards killed off the "Indians," they didn't mystically disappear or die of diptheria.

Trey wrote his critique as a letter to Allyn and Bacon, publishers of *The American Spirit:*

. . . I'll just pick one topic to keep it simple. How about Columbus. No, you didn't lie, but saying, "Though they had a keen interest in the peoples of the Caribbean, Columbus and his crews were never able to live peacefully among them," makes it seem as if Columbus did no wrong. The reason for not being able to live peacefully is that he and his crew took slaves, and killed thousands of Indians for not bringing enough gold. . . .

If I were to only know the information given in this book, I would have such a sheltered viewpoint that many of my friends would think I was stupid. Later in life people could capitalize on my ignorance by comparing Columbus's voyage with something similar, but in our time. I wouldn't believe the ugly truths brought up by the opposition because it is just like Columbus, and he did no harm, I've known that since the eighth grade.

Keely chose the same book, which happens to be the text adopted by Portland Public Schools, where I teach:

. . . I found that the facts left in were, in fact, facts. There was nothing made up. Only things left out. There was one sentence in the whole section where Indians were mentioned. And this was only to say why Columbus called them "Indians." Absolutely nothing was said about slaves or gold. . . .

The book, as I said, doesn't mention the Indians really, so of course you're on Christopher's side. They say how he falls to his knees and thanks God for saving him and his crew and for making their voyage successful.

After students have read and discussed their papers in small groups we ask them to reflect on the papers as a whole and write about our collective text: What did they discover about textbook treatments of Columbus? Here are some excerpts. Matthew wrote:

As people read their evaluations the same situations in these textbooks came out. Things were conveniently left out so that you sided with Columbus's quest to "boldly go where no man has gone before". . . None of the harsh violent reality is confronted in these so-called true accounts.

Gina tried to account for why the books were so consistently rosy:

It seemed to me as if the publishers had just printed up some "glory story" that was supposed to make us feel more patriotic about our country. In our group, we talked about the possibility of the government trying to protect young students from such violence. We soon decided that that was probably one of the farthest things from their minds. They want us to look at our country as great, and powerful, and forever right. They want us to believe Columbus was a real hero. We're being fed lies. We don't question the facts, we just absorb information that is handed to us because we trust the role models that are handing it out.

Rebecca's collective text reflected the general tone of disillusion with the official story of textbooks:

Of course, the writers of the books probably think it's harmless enough—what does it matter who discovered America, really, and besides it makes them feel good about America. But the thought that I have been lied to all my life about this, and who knows what else, really makes me angry.

The reflections on the collective text became the basis for a class discussion of these and other issues. Again and again, students blasted their textbooks for consistently making choices that left readers with inadequate, and ultimately untruthful, understandings. And while we didn't press to arrive at definitive explanations for the omissions and distortions, we did seek to underscore the contemporary abuses of historical ignorance. If the books wax romantic about Columbus planting the flag on island beaches and taking possession of land occupied by naked red-skinned Indians, what do young readers learn from this about today's world? That white people have a right to dominate peoples of color? That might—or wealth—makes right? That it's justified to take people's land if you are more "civilized" or have a "better" religion? Whatever the answers, the textbooks condition students to accept some form of inequality; nowhere do the books suggest that the Indians were, or even should have been, sovereign peoples with a right to control their own lands. And if Columbus' motives for exploration are mystified or ignored, then students are less apt to look beyond today's pious explanations for U.S. involvements in, say, Central America or the Middle East. As Bobby, approaching his registration day for the military draft, pointed out in class: "If people thought they were going off to war to fight for profits, maybe they wouldn't fight as well, or maybe they wouldn't go."

It's important to note that some students are left troubled from these myth-popping discussions. One student wrote that she was "left not knowing who to believe." Josh was the most articulate in his skepticism. He had begun to "read" our class from the same critical distance from which we hoped students would approach textbooks:

I still wonder. . . . If we can't believe what our first grade teachers told us, why should we believe you? If they lied to us, why wouldn't you? If one book is wrong, why isn't another?

What is your purpose in telling us about how awful Chris was?
What interest do you have in telling us the truth? What is it you
want from us?

What indeed? It was a wonderfully probing series of questions and Linda and I responded by reading them (anonymously)
to the entire class. We asked students to take a few minutes to
write additional questions and comments on the Columbus
activities or to try to imagine our response as teachers—what
was the point of our lessons?

We hoped students would see that the intent of the unit was
to present a whole new way of reading, and ultimately of
experiencing, the world. Textbooks fill students with information masquerading as final truth and then ask students to
parrot back the information in end-of-the-chapter "checkups."

The Brazilian educator Paulo Freire calls it the "banking
method": students are treated as empty vessels waiting for
deposits of wisdom from textbooks and teachers.[8] We wanted
to assert to students that they shouldn't necessarily trust the
"authorities," but instead need to be active participants in their
own learning, peering between lines for unstated assumptions
and unasked questions. Meaning is something *they* need to
create, individually and collectively.

Josh asked what our "interest" was in this kind of education
and it's a fair, even vital, question. Linda and I see teaching as
political action: we want to equip students to build a truly
democratic society. As Freire writes, to be an actor for social
change one must "read the word and the world."[9] We hope
that if a student is able to maintain a critical distance from the
written word, then it's possible to maintain that same distance
from one's society: to stand back, look hard and ask, "Why is
it like this, how can I make it better?"

Postscript

As the final assignment in our unit on Native American history, Linda and I asked students to create a project that would reach beyond the walls of the classroom to educate others in the school or larger community. As a class we had uncovered multiple layers of a twisted and biased history. We worried that unless we offered students a chance to act on these new understandings, the unintended subtext or "hidden curriculum" embedded in our teaching was a cynical one: your role as students is to uncover injustice, not to do anything about it.

We told students the form their projects took didn't matter: the only requirement was that each of them would make some kind of presentation to others outside the classroom. And they took us at our word. One group of aspiring musicians produced a raucous rock video about the damming of the Columbia River which drowned the ancient fishing grounds of the Celilo Indians. Another group choreographed and performed for other classes a dance, at the same time bitter and humorous, on Columbus's "discovery" and search for gold. Several students interviewed local Northwest Indian tribal leaders about their struggle over fishing rights on the Columbia River. The group produced a video tape subsequently broadcast over the school's closed-circuit TV news show.

One young woman, Nicole Smith, wrote and illustrated a children's book, *Chris*. In the story, a young boy named Christopher moves from his old Spain Street neighborhood to a new house on Salvadora Street. He's miserable and misses his old friends, Ferdie and Isie. While wandering the new neighborhood he spots a colorful playhouse and declares, "I claim this clubhouse in the name of me, and my best friends Ferdie and Isie." The rightful owners of the clubhouse soon return and confront Christopher, who insists that the structure is now *his* because he "discovered" it. "How can you come here and discover something that we built and really care about?" the boys demand. The story ends happily when they agree to let Christopher share the clubhouse if he helps with the upkeep—a metaphorical twist that would have been nice five hundred years earlier.

Linda arranged for Nicole to read her story to a number of classes in a local elementary school. She opened each session by asking if anyone had something with which to write. When an unsuspecting youngster volunteered a pencil, Nicole thanked the student, then pocketed it. This elementary school version of purse-stealing gave Nicole a handy introduction to the theft-posing-as-discovery lesson in her short story.

Like Rebecca and many other students, Nicole was angry she had been lied to about Columbus and the genocide of indigenous people in the Caribbean. However, the final project assignment encouraged her to channel that anger in an activist direction. She became a teacher, offering the youngsters a framework in which to locate and question the romanticized textbook patter about "exploration" and "discovery," providing a hoped-for innoculation against the lies and omissions they will be sure to encounter in their schooling. Nicole's story and lesson were a kind of revenge: getting back at those who miseducated her so many years before. But as she was teaching she was also learning—learning that the best way to address injustice is to work for change.

Notes

1. *The Annals of America, Volume 1: 1493-1754, Discovering a New World* (Chicago: Encyclopedia Britannica, 1968), pp. 2, 4.

2. Quoted in Hans Koning, *Columbus: His Enterprise,* p. 53. As Koning points out, none of the information included in his book is new. It is available in Columbus' own journals and letters and the writings of the Spanish priest Bartolomé de las Casas. Even Columbus' adoring biographers admit the Admiral's outrages. For example, Pulitzer Prize winner Samuel Eliot Morison acknowledges that Columbus unleashed savage dogs on Indians, kidnapped Indian leaders, and encouraged his sailors to rape Indian women. At one point Morison writes, "The cruel policy initiated by Columbus and pursued by his successors resulted in complete genocide." See Samuel Eliot Morison, *Christopher Columbus, Mariner* (New York: New American Library, 1942), p. 99. But the sharpness of this judgment is buried in Morison's syrupy admiration for Columbus' courage and navigational skills.

3. Koning, *Columbus,* p. 83; emphasis in original.

4. Ibid., pp. 83–84.

5. It's useful to keep in mind the distinction between cynicism and skepticism. As Norman Diamond writes, "In an important respect, the two are not even commensurable. Skepticism says, 'You'll have to show me, otherwise I'm dubious'; it is open to engagement and persuasion. . . . Cynicism is a removed perspective, a renunciation of any responsibility." See Norman Diamond, "Against Cynicism in Politics and Culture," in *Monthly Review* 28, no. 2 (June 1976): 40.

6. Edna McGuire, *The Story of American Freedom* (New York: The Macmillan Company, 1964), p. 24.

7. Ibid., p. 26.

8. See Paulo Freire, *Pedagogy of the Oppressed* (New York: Continuum, 1970). This banking method of education, Freire writes (p.

58), ". . .turns [students] into 'receptacles' to be 'filled' by the teacher. . . .

"Education thus becomes an act of depositing, in which the students are depositories and the teacher is the depositor. Instead of communicating, the teacher issues communiques and makes deposits which the students patiently receive, memorize, and repeat. This is the 'banking' concept of education, in which the scope of action allowed to the students extends only as far as receiving, filing, and storing the deposits. They do, it is true, have the opportunity to become collectors or cataloguers of the things they store. But in the last analysis, it is men [people] themselves who are filed away through the lack of creativity, transformation, and knowledge in this (at best) misguided system."

9. Paulo Freire and Donaldo Macedo, *Literacy: Reading the Word and the World* (South Hadley, MA: Bergin and Garvey, 1987).

ABOUT THE AUTHORS

Hans Koning was born Hans Koningsberger in Amsterdam, Holland. He fought against the Nazis and after the war ended up in the United States, arriving on a freighter from Indonesia. He has written eleven novels and five works of nonfiction. Some of his best-known books are *The Affair, A Walk with Love and Death,* and *Death of a Schoolboy*. He is prominent in the activities of Columbus-In-Context, a national grassroots organization devoted to commemorating rather than celebrating the Quincentennial of 1492. He has written about their aim of "rethinking five hundred years of American history" in the *New York Times* and other national newspapers. He currently lives in New Haven, Connecticut.

Bill Bigelow is the author of two curricula, one on South Africa and the other, with Norman Diamond, entitled *The Power in Our Hands: A Curriculum on the History of Work and Workers in the United States* (Monthly Review Press, 1988). He teaches at Jefferson High School in Portland, Oregon, and is active in Columbus-In-Context.